N

British Library Cataloguing-in-Publication Data
A catalogue record for this book is available from the
British Library

Norwich Canaries

by

C. A. HOUSE and A. W. SMITH

A clear buff Norwich Plainhead Canary hen of ideal exhibition type

CONTENTS

EDITOR'S FOREWORD

PROBABLY no variety of Canary has been subjected to so many changes and vicissitudes as the Norwich Plainhead. Eighty years ago, and earlier, it was the most widely kept breed, both in fanciers' birdrooms and in the living rooms of great and humble homes.

The cultivation of this Canary as a distinct variety is said to have begun during the latter part of the sixteenth century. That was the time when numbers of Flemish weavers, fleeing from Spanish persecution, sought refuge in England. Many of these refugees settled down in the county of Norfolk, where they found congenial employment in the worsted industry, started two centuries earlier by their ancestors. At this period, Canary breeding had become a popular pursuit throughout Germany; it was also extensively engaged in by the peasants of the Netherlands. Naturally, therefore, a good proportion of these settlers brought their stocks of Canaries with them, and for many years the breed was propagated in the city of Norwich, as well as in the surrounding districts.

To-day this old variety is enjoying immense popularity. Breeders have evolved an up-to-date type of Plainhead, a bird of exquisite shape, noble in head, and with short feather which renders it immune against the trouble known as " lumps," a feather disease brought about largely by the introduction of the

Crested Norwich cross which increased length of feather to an inordinate degree. This affliction caused a serious setback in popularity some twenty-five years ago, but present-day breeders, by careful selection of pairs, have done much to ensure that no repetition of the trouble shall occur.

Newcomers to the Canary Fancy are strongly recommended to take up the cultivation of the Norwich Plainhead. It is a handsome variety, by no means difficult to breed, and classes are provided on a generous scale at most of the open exhibitions.

E. R. W. LINCOLN,
Editor of CAGE BIRDS.

PART I by C. A. HOUSE

CHAPTER I

NORWICH CANARIES

MANY years have slipped by since I exhibited my first Norwich Plainhead Canary. Over a long period I was never without a few good specimens in my bird-room. In those days Norwich Plainheads were the most popular Canaries on the show bench and in the home. But they were very different in appearance from the present-day type of Plainhead which is so immensely attractive.

Originally the Norwich Plainhead was a smart little Canary about the size of a modern Border Fancy. To give my readers some idea of the change which the years have wrought, I may say that in size and shape the Norwich and Lizard Canary of some eighty years back were very much alike; in fact, the two breeds were often crossed, the Norwich men using the Lizard to improve the colour and quality of feather.

As the Lizard is now, so was the Norwich then, a bird of about five and a quarter to five and a half inches in length. To-day the length set out in the standards of the various Norwich specialist clubs is six and a half inches. A proportion of outstanding winners exceeds this length, but there is now a concerted move among our best breeders to keep the bird as short and compact as possible, consistent with the maintenance of other show characteristics.

During the years following the first world war there seemed to be a mania for producing Plainheads of exceptional size. Certain breeders " swept the decks " with exhibits which were stouter, deeper and longer than anything seen before. With this apparent increase in size, not of a structural nature, but brought about by grossly excessive feather, came other features of a far from desirable character, and the soft, sleek, silky jackets which Norwich of earlier date possessed were lost for a time. Since then, however, breeders have seen the " red light." They no longer have any use for the ultra-heavily feathered, browy monstrosity which was largely responsible for the severe outbreak of " lumps " during 1918 and subsequent years.

In the early days of which I write, out of the hundred points which went to make up the ideal bird in the official standard of excellence, forty-five were given to colour alone, and, as if this allocation were insufficient, twenty more were added for extra good sheen and brilliance. Eight points only were given for size, and a mere six for shape.

To-day the standards of the Norwich Plainhead Clubs allocate fifty-five points for size and shape, that is type, and ten for colour. Thus, instead of being, as it was, principally a bird of colour, the Norwich is now a type bird and must be so judged.

Again, in those far-off times only fifteen points were allowed for condition and quality. Nowadays they stand equal, if not in front of, colour, or should do so. Unfortunately, some judges, mostly the older ones, still give preference to colour over type, but this can-

The birds here portrayed were regarded as ideal Norwich Plainheads during the middle part of the nineteenth century. (Left to right) : A variegated yellow, evenly-marked yellow, and a clear buff.

not be said of the younger adjudicators. Anyway, these fundamental changes which have taken place in assessing the merits of exhibition Plainheads are so remarkable that one can hardly credit their occurrence among a body of men so conservative as cage bird fanciers.

These changes have not been caused by any sudden revulsion of feeling. Movement towards the modern ideal has been very gradual indeed. It was in the year 1887 that the first of the really big birds was seen in the South of England. This was a cock which came from the stud of a Hampshire breeder who turned out many a good Norwich in the days that are past. The bird to which I refer was called " The Wonder," and he was well named, for he did, indeed, make the Fancy wonder. Judges and prominent exhibitors were shaken when they first saw " The Wonder," at Ipswich show towards the close of 1887. They all declared that the bird was not a Norwich at all. Mr. Joseph Bexson, that famous judge who was officiating at this particular Ipswich fixture, thought otherwise, and he placed " The Wonder " first. He liked big specimens.

Myself, I have never been able to see anything attractive about these big, slovenly, heavily feathered birds. A Norwich should be short and cobby in body, close and short in feather. Why, then, do some judges and exhibitors still go against the standard?

Generally speaking, when any forward movement is in the making, the men of the North not only have a big share in it, but generally take the lead. So it was in this matter of big Norwich. They soon began to give the judges something to look at, which, so far as size was concerned, resembled a cross between a Thrush and a Bullfinch.

From Lancashire came these big birds, and in plenty, too, the chief breeding centres being Prescot, St. Helens, and Liverpool, the former taking the lead. " A real good Prescot Norwich " was the highest form of praise that a Northern breeder of the later 'eighties could bestow upon any bird. Those Prescot birds were big in body, that is, deep, wide and round, but they were not long in feather or shape. Some birds shown at the present time are still too long in body and in feather

Plainheads were exhibited in open wire show cages at Lancashire shows during the 'eighties, not in the box cages which are now universally seen. Lancashire breeders were wedded to these open wire cages, and it was many years before they discarded them altogether. These cages were longer and broader than those now in use by Yorkshire breeders, but were not so high. I cannot say that they were cages to admire, but they certainly possessed one great advantage—a judge could see all over a bird at once.

Not only in the style and form of their cages have Norwich breeders of the North made advance; they have also improved the shape and quality of their birds. Prescot held the lead when the big birds were asked for, and it has held the lead many a time since. In addition to size they also had type in their studs. Prescot Norwich of those days were definitely chubby in shape, and from the town famous for its electrical and watch equipment works have come some of the most typical Norwich of modern days, descendants from those big birds of long ago.

The men of the North carried the craze for size too far, and a reaction set in among the men of the East, the West, and the South. Agitation and correspondence in the papers of that time led to the calling together of the famous conference at the Crystal Palace in February, 1890. At this historical gathering it was said that between three hundred and four hundred breeders from the city of Norwich were present, while other parts of the country were also well represented. The result of that conference was that a new standard was decided upon, and since then type has had greater consideration than it had previously.

It was there decided that in future the Norwich Plainhead should be judged more for type, and the length was limited to six and a half inches so as to shut out the long-sided, coarse-feathered birds, whose overhanging eyebrows and shaggy thighs gave evidence of Crest blood running in their veins.

Type! This was the battle-cry, a cry taken up by the Norwich Plainhead Club which was afterwards formed, and, thanks in very great measure to the action of that club, type has been, and is to-day, accorded greater prominence. But good judges never fail to give due consideration to quality of feather—and size, if consistent with correct type.

The efforts of the Norwich Plainhead Club have been admirably backed up by the Scottish Norwich Plainhead Club, the Norwich Plainhead Canary Club, and the Southern Norwich Plainhead Canary Club, all of which specialist societies have a strong, forceful, and growing membership, and are yearly becoming stronger.

Evolution is, we are told, continually going on in the world around us. There is no standing still. New types and new forms are being evolved in every direction, and when one looks back to the 'seventies and 'eighties of the last century, one sees many changes in the Norwich Plainhead Fancy.

At that time the city of Norwich was the great stronghold of the breed, and exhibitors from everywhere used to flock to its annual show to buy birds for exhibition. No longer is this the case. No longer do all the cups and specials migrate eastwards. Although there are still quite a number of breeders in East Anglia, they have not to-day a monopoly of good stock.

If a census could be taken now we should probably find that Norwich are raised in good numbers throughout the country. There are plenty in the Midlands; that is, in the Northampton, Coventry and Nottingham districts. The breed is also strongly cultivated in and around London, in Scotland, Cambridgeshire, Cornwall, and in the Southern Counties. From all these areas fine Plainheads are forthcoming each season.

The popularity of the Norwich is unquestionably more widespread than ever before in its history. Moreover, it has become an established favourite with fellow-fanciers in many parts of the Commonwealth (particularly Australia, South Africa and Canada), in the United States of America, and in various European countries.

It can truthfully be said that to-day the " evolution " of a few decades ago has taken on a form pleasing to every eye. Though the bird remains much larger than it was in its early days, size is no longer synonymous with length of body and a plethora of feather.

The Norwich Plainhead is still $6\frac{1}{2}$-in. long, but has thickened in build of body, stoutness of neck and boldness of head, and is clothed in silky feather that fits to perfection—a worthy " John Bull " of the Fancy.

CHAPTER II

THE BREEDING-ROOM AND CAGES

IT is an axiom among athletes that a good start is half the race. The same thing applies in the Cage Bird Fancy, and the reason why many fail to gain high honours on the exhibition bench is because they start badly. A good start may not ensure a successful finish, but it will go a long way towards it. There is an old proverb which speaks of getting the cage before the bird, and a very wise piece of advice it is.

In the breeding-room the practical side of things should be fully considered. Ornamental cages, while eminently suitable for the drawing-room, are quite out of place in the breeding-room. But I am getting somewhat ahead of my subject. The first thought should be a suitable room, then the cages, and finally the birds.

As to the room, it is very often a matter of Hobson's choice, and not being able to have the most suitable room in the house, the Canary breeder must, perforce, take the one which can be best spared.

When choice can be exercised, however, a room with a south-east aspect should be selected. Never choose a room which faces due east, if it can be avoided. A room facing due south should also be avoided, as in such a room the heat in summer time will be almost unbearable. With a south-east aspect the birds get the early morning light, and they escape the full force of the sun during the heat of the day.

16

A bird-room should contain nothing but what is needful and useful to the birds. Do not keep anything in it that is not wanted, as the more there is in the room the more there will be to keep clean, and we all know how soon dust and dirt accumulate in a bird-room.

The floor should be covered with floorcloth or

Outdoor room neatly fitted up with four tiers of breeding cages containing high-class Plainhead pairs. Norwich show cages are seen in the background.

linoleum, so that waste seed and dirt are easily swept up. The floor should be washed at least once a week. This is not a nice job for one not used to it, and it generally means that female assistance has to be called in.

Birds rejoice in fresh air, therefore give them plenty of it. Do not be afraid to have the room well ventilated. There is seldom a day when the windows may not be opened. During the greater part of the year they should be open night and day, and even in the depth of winter they should be open daily for a few moments.

Fresh air is most essential to the birds' welfare, and their owner's success. To protect one's pets from cats, and to prevent the birds from escaping, a wire frame should be attached to the inside of the window frames.

If success is to be attained and a correct record kept of all birds bred, each pair must have a separate domicile provided for them. Let me say right away that I am a firm believer in single pairing. The cage I recommend is the single breeder type, just a plain box with a wire front. Such a cage, when properly made and painted, affords little harbour for red mite. It is handy and get-at-able for all purposes, and will be found to be generally convenient.

In size it should be not less than eighteen inches long, eighteen inches in height, and eleven inches in depth from front to back. The door should be in the centre, and there should be holes on each side of the doorway so that the birds may reach their food and water. The main stay should be fitted with a couple of china or enamelled egg-food pans; they are much better than tins. This, with the necessary perches, seed hopper, and drinking vessel, make the cage complete.

Many experienced fanciers prefer to use a double breeding cage, which is approximately twice the length of a single breeder with a central partition of wood. The advantages of a cage of this type are fairly obvious. In the first place, any cock bird which makes a nuisance of himself during the rearing season can easily be transferred to the unoccupied compartment, either by with-

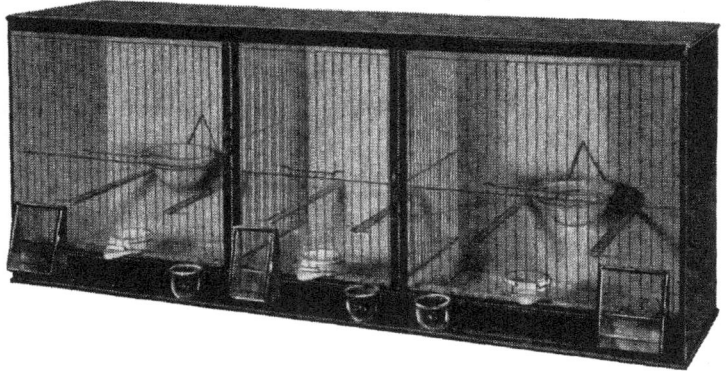

Triple breeding cage equipped with two movable slides which proves useful when a fancier wishes to run a cock bird with two hens. Remove both slides and you have an excellent flight cage 60 in. in length. Note the correct positioning of the perches below nest-rim level.

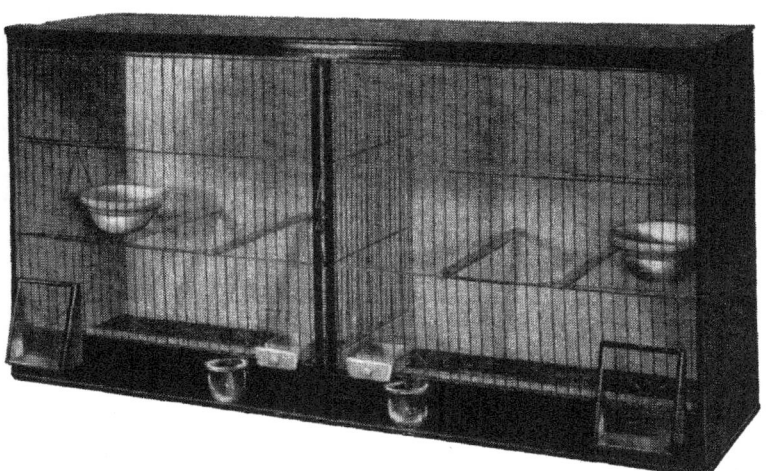

Double breeding cage with a central removable slide. Suitable for one pair, or two pairs when the slide is in position. The illustration shows the cage fitted up as two single breeders.

drawing the partition slightly or by opening up the circular hole which is cut in the upper portion of it.

Secondly, the alternative compartment can be used as a nursery for partially weaned babies which can be fed by the parents through the wires of a metal partition substituted for the wooden one, when this becomes desirable. Thirdly, with the partition removed altogether a double breeding cage makes quite a satisfactory flight cage. In some bird-rooms three-compartment cages are to be seen, and these, of course, provide really excellent flight cages when the *two* partitions are withdrawn.

Drinkers and Drawboards

For drinking purposes I always recommend open glass vessels, which are easily secured by a wire band fixed in the front of the main stay. These glasses are easily cleaned. On the question of the drawboard, or turn-rail, I vote for the drawboard. It can be easily removed for cleaning purposes, and it keeps the bottom of the cage from becoming foul.

Clean the cages out at least once a week, and every day when young are being fed. Some fanciers use sawdust for the bottom of the cages, but I prefer sand. I know this comes rather expensive to buy, but it is more suitable for the birds than sawdust, and does not get blown about the room, neither does it cause trouble if it gets into the insides of the young birds. Sand aids digestion, sawdust prevents it, and many young birds die every year because sawdust gets mixed in with their food.

If single breeders only are used, flight cages of good length will be needed once there are young birds about, therefore it is wise to provide them at the same time as the breeding cages. By so doing, the room can be properly planned and equipped and made to have a neat and uniform appearance.

As to the fixing of the cages, racks are best for the purpose, and each cage should be made to rest on four brass studs driven into the framework. This will allow a free current of air over and under each cage, and also prevent red mite from finding refuge.

All egg and seed pans used inside the cage should be of white china or enamel. The drinking vessels, which should always be outside the cage, should be of glass. In the way of nest pans, either earthenware, or wooden ones with perforated zinc bottoms, can be used.

When I first became interested in Canary breeding it was the universal practice to whitewash all breeding cages. To-day it is not so. The majority of fanciers in these times either paint, enamel or creosote their cages. Of these three substances I prefer leadless paint, though I must admit that creosote is very satisfactory, even if plain wood cages so treated do not look attractive.

Canaries which are of a prying, inquisitive nature are always pecking about. Therefore, unless enamel is very carefully and very efficiently put on, there is a possibility that they may get hold of a lump, swallow it, and then succumb to an attack of inflammation.

Before painting the cages, all cracks and crevices should be attended to with a view to eliminating any hiding-places for red mite. Fill up every crack and crevice, after applying the first coat of paint, with putty made as follows: Get some whiting or lime that has been slacked for some time and is almost as fine as flour. Put this in the oven and dry off every bit of moisture. Then add boiled linseed oil, and work it up to the consistency of ordinary putty. This will set as hard as stone, and will not shrink like the commercial article.

Remember, before putting birds into cages that have been newly painted, to examine the appliances thoroughly, and be quite certain the paint is hard and dry.

The great advantage of painting a cage is that it is so easy to wash out at any time when that operation is needful, and should infectious disease break out, cages which are painted inside and out cannot absorb or hold infection like those which are unpainted. Sky blue is as good as any colour for the inside of the cages, while the outside, wire included, should be black.

There are few fanciers who give sufficient thought to perches. No perch should be less than half an inch wide and three-eighths of an inch deep. Small perches of about the circumference of a lead pencil are an abomination. They are a constant source of trouble. Many cases of cramp, sore feet, broken joints and toe nails are due to their use.

Fanciers who make a study of their birds are fully alive to the evils of small perches. The greatest offenders are those persons who keep one or two birds for singing only. It should be remembered that birds, like men, have feet of different sizes, and one standard size of perch is not advisable. Birds with large feet require larger perches than those with smaller ones, and *vice versa*.

Further, all the perches need not be, and should not be, of the same size. It affords ease to the birds to be able to settle on perches of different sizes. Have two sets of perches, so that when one is in use the other can be cleaned. The best and quickest way to clean them is to place them in a bath and pour boiling water on them; then scrub them and let them get thoroughly dry before you put them back in the cages.

Outdoor Birdrooms

If it is quite impossible to have a room in the dwelling-house, space may be found in the yard or garden for a bird-house. I have seen many excellent bird-houses in small yards attached to town houses, and in the gardens of suburban residences.

Large outdoor Canary room with good ventilation and an abundance of illumination. A great number of breeding cages are arranged in tiers along the back of the building, the entry door to which is located in the centre.

Such a house should be made of fairly substantial deal, grooved and tongued for the outside, and, if at all possible, an inside lining of five-eighths boards should be used. This would leave a space of about two or two and a half inches between the outer and

Distinctive style of outdoor room which is most pleasing to the eye. Apart from the unusual method of providing top lighting, a noteworthy feature is the covered flight on the right.

inner boards, which should be filled up with sawdust. The outside variations of temperature will then have little effect upon the bird-room. The roof should also be double-cased and covered either with felt or corrugated iron.

The dimensions and strength of the timber used in such a house must depend, of course, upon the number of cages it is going to accommodate. The larger the house the stronger must be the timber used in the framework, because of the greater strain upon it. The floor should be of inch boards tongued and grooved.

In the construction of an outdoor room care must be taken to provide plenty of ventilation, and this should be contrived by means of adequate intake and outlet ventilators, the former at or about floor level. The house should be raised eighteen inches from the ground so as to allow of a free current of air underneath. This will prevent dry-rot setting in, keep the house dry, and stop the entry of rats and mice.

There are several distinct advantages attaching to an outdoor Canary breeding-room. In the first place, it is often possible to arrange that it has a more or less ideal aspect. Secondly, lighting and ventilation can be arranged in an almost perfect manner when careful attention is paid to these two important items.

Thirdly, one does not have to climb up and down stairs, as in the case of the bird-room in the dwelling, and fourthly, no exasperation is caused by seed being scattered about in a garden room. Everything considered, therefore, a well-constructed, cosy, draught-proof outside place is preferable to one indoors.

Many modern outdoor bird-rooms are equipped with thermostatically controlled electric heaters, and these appliances are invaluable during the early part of the breeding season. The breeder has only to set his thermostatic control, and he can keep the bird-room within a degree or two of the desired temperature night and day, irrespective of outdoor fluctuations. These heating appliances, judiciously used, go a long way to prevent egg-binding during March and April nesting.

CHAPTER III

BREEDING TIME

IF there is one thing more than another upon which the success or failure of a stud of birds depends it is in the selecting of the original breeding stock. It is the most difficult task a beginner has to face, and he should, if possible, always seek expert guidance in his early selections. If unhealthy stock birds are mated it is impossible to rear strong, healthy young.

When starting, it is wise to go to some known breeder and ask him to select breeding birds for you. Tell him how much you have to spend, and trust to his honour to do his best for you. The most suitable time to acquire stock is at the end of the moulting season, about the end of September, or the beginning of October. The birds then have the whole winter during which to settle down and become thoroughly accustomed to their new home before they are called upon to commence parental duties.

Birds should not be mated unless they are perfectly fit. This can be ascertained by their movements. Birds in breeding form are continually hopping from perch to perch, flapping their wings, and calling to one another. The best time to pair, all things being ready, is the end of March or the beginning of April. Between that date and the early part of July there is ample time to take three nests, which is as many as should be taken in one season.

When the birds are paired they should be fed in a

liberal manner. The seed hoppers should always be well supplied with canary seed, and twice a day they should have egg-food, to which a little brown sugar has been added. The sugar acts as a preventive of egg-binding. Half a teaspoonful of hemp or niger may also be offered to each bird every other day. A sprig or two of watercress or other green food should also be given daily.

When the birds have been together a few days the nest-box and a little nesting material, such as dried grass, moss and cowhair, should be introduced. Do not provide a lot of it, for the birds will only mess it about and soil it. If they are fit they will soon get to work at nest-building, and when you see they mean business you can easily give them more material. Within a few days of the nest being completed the hen may be expected to lay.

In fixing the nest, care should be taken not to have it too high or too low, but at such a height that the birds may stand on the perch and feed the young. When the nest is fixed close up to the top of the cage the eggs are often infertile. Many birds pair on the nest edge, and, therefore, the nest should not be poked into a corner or be fixed too high up. It occasionally happens that a hen builds her nest on the floor and will not use the nest-box. In such cases place the nest-box on the floor and put the nest into it.

The eggs, which are usually laid in the morning between seven and eight, should be removed soon after they are produced, dummies being substituted. It is wise to have a box containing as many divisions as there are breeding cages in the room. Each division should be filled with soft material and numbered to correspond with the numbers of the breeding cages. By this means the eggs will be kept distinct, and the parentage and pedigree of every bird bred will be known.

It is the general practice to return the eggs on the evening of the day on which the third is laid, and on the fourteenth day of incubation the young may be expected to hatch out. Never handle the eggs; lift them with a teaspoon. When they are returned to the nest they should be given a slight dusting with insect powder.

From the time when the young are hatched the parent birds should have additional soft food given to them. Soaked seed is also most valuable at this time, and a regular and plentiful supply of green food should be offered daily. Much harm can be done by undue interference with the nestlings, and it is wise never to interfere with the hen while on the nest, and only to look at the young when she is off feeding.

Fanciers should make a practice of looking round the room the last thing at night and the first thing in the morning just to make sure that all is going on well. If this is done the life of many a youngster will be saved, for by carrying out such inspections one can ascertain if the parents are attending to their babes properly. Should it be that they are not feeding well, then hand-feeding must be resorted to. It sometimes happens that a hen will not feed for the first day or two, yet afterwards make a most exemplary parent.

I am a firm believer in soaked seed for feeding hens. I have known hens who at once showed much greater interest in rearing their nestlings upon being given some soaked seed. The best way to prepare such seed is to utilize a basin or jar. A jam pot is most useful and handy.

Place in it equal quantities of canary, rape and hemp seed, cover with cold water, let it soak twelve hours, then stir well, strain off, and cover again with fresh water. Let it soak for another twelve hours, then stir again, rinse with fresh water, strain off, and it is ready to use. To keep a regular supply going, the seed for the morning feed should be put in soak the morning before, and that for the evening feed the evening before.

Wholemeal Bread Preferred

When it comes to preparing egg-food, I prefer wholemeal bread to biscuits. A slice is placed in a basin of water for a quarter of an hour, then squeezed dry and mixed with one egg. The whole may be put through a small sieve or a potato squeezer.

Most fanciers use one or other of the prepared foods which are advertised in CAGE BIRDS, and these proprietary products are quite excellent. Such foods contain all the nutriment required, with the addition of hard-boiled egg-yolk finely minced up. In the preparation of all soft food everything used should be scrupulously clean, and feeding vessels should be scalded every time after use.

Although not advocating too much handling of the young birds, I think it advisable to change the nest when the youngsters are seven or eight days old. If lined nests are used, all that is needed is to take out the old nest, transfer the youngsters, and hang up the new nest. But if the old-fashioned, wooden nest-box is used, some nesting material should be placed in a clean box and modelled into shape with a heated-up egg.

Before transferring the young, sprinkle the new nest with a good insecticide powder. The old nest should not be left in the room, but should be taken away and burnt, while the nest-box or pan should be placed in boiling water.

Birds which are in robust health will go to nest a second time when the first brood is about three weeks old. Thus it is well for the owner to anticipate events by placing a clean nest pan and some nesting material inside the cage. If this is done they will not be so likely to pluck their young, a practice which if once started is difficult to cure.

To Minimize Plucking

It is also advisable during the breeding season to keep a piece of hempen rope tied to the wires of the front. This is a good preventive of plucking. Should the hen go to nest again before the young birds are old enough to look after themselves, the cock can usually be depended upon to attend to them. When they are a month old they will be able to fend for themselves.

At this age they can be removed to a flight cage, where they should get their soft food for another fortnight. Wean them on to a seed diet gradually by reducing the quantity of egg-food and soaked seed. They should never be put on hard seed all at once.

When they can crack whole seed they will require little attention till the moulting season comes round, but keep a watchful eye on them. Clean, sound seed, plenty of fresh water for bathing and drinking, a liberal supply of good grit and cuttlefish bone, fresh air and exercise are all that they need to keep healthy and strong.

The expected difficulties which crop up during the rearing season do not worry old breeders unduly, but to the novice, any setbacks that occur cause him con-

The purpose of this illustration is to show how perches should *not* be fitted. They are placed above the nest, and this may cause the hen to leap out and drag an unfortunate nestling with her.

siderable anxiety and vexation. A common experience is a young bird being thrown out of the nest. If this happens, place the young bird in the hand and breathe repeatedly upon it. If it revives, place it under the hen and in a short time it will be little the worse for the experience.

It is sometimes necessary to resort to hand-feeding owing to the parents neglecting their duty. When this occurs the young birds should be placed with other hens which have young. If this cannot be done, it is scarcely worth trying to bring them up by hand. Hand-rearing is a wearisome and unprofitable occupation as a rule, because success so seldom attends one's efforts. Therefore, unless the nestlings are bred from birds of exceptional value I would not advise it being undertaken.

For those who wish to hand-feed, the following is the *modus operandi*: Take a small quantity of yolk of egg and an equal quantity of Osborne (or similar) biscuit, and mix with a little milk to the consistency of fresh cream. The birds should be fed with this mixture every two hours from sunrise to sunset by means of a " Filup " or similar kind of feeder.

Reluctance on the part of some hens to rear their nestlings can be attributed to many obscure causes. With many of them it is due to sheer nervousness. For this reason it is always a good plan to mate up an old cock with a nervous young hen. His presence often has a reassuring effect.

On the question of taking the cock away while the hen is sitting, there is great diversity of opinion. Much depends on the temperament of the birds. Personally, I am against it. I never remove him unless he interferes with the hen. A good, reliable cock is of great value, as youngsters seldom go wrong when their sire gives them the necessary attention.

The only time I think it advisable to remove him is when a hen is " sweating " her young. The hen, having all the responsibility of the family placed upon her, will sometimes rise to the occasion, and having constantly to leave her nest, the so-called sweating ceases.

Nothing is more disappointing than the non-hatching of fertile eggs. The causes are various and include lack of moisture, failure of the hen to turn them in the nest, and lack of vigour in the parents.

The daily use of the bath will prevent the first mentioned, and a well-shaped nest will obviate the second; but the third, unfortunately, cannot be remedied, though it can be prevented by making sure that the stock birds are thoroughly strong and healthy. If the nest-box is exposed to the glare of the light the hen will only sit in one direction, but if it is shaded, then she will constantly reverse her position and move the eggs.

Damaged Eggs and Slipped Claws

It sometimes happens that eggs are cracked or chipped during incubation. The cause is generally long claws or dirt adhering to the feet through the bath not being given often enough, or the cage not being kept clean.

" Slip claw " is another trouble. It can generally be cured if taken in hand as soon as the birds leave the nest. The best method is to fasten the claw back to the leg with a small piece of india-rubber tubing such as is used for babies' feeding bottles. Another device to assist weak-clawed birds or those with " slip claws " is a perch triangular in shape.

During the breeding season, red mite make their appearance in many rooms, but in the majority of cases the owners are themselves to blame for not keeping the cages and nests scrupulously clean. If the cages are well cleaned, plenty of insect powder used in the nests, and the perches scrubbed each week, the ends being dipped in turpentine or methylated spirits before being returned, there will not be much trouble from red mite.

Shell-less eggs are caused sometimes by weakness in the hen, sometimes by fright, and sometimes because the birds are not supplied with suitable grit and shell-making material. Birds intended for breeding should be given plenty of shell, gravel, cuttlefish bone, and pulverised oyster-shell, not only during the breeding season, but also some time before being mated.

Hens which are at all delicate and lay shell-less eggs should be given a rest. It is also advisable to dissolve a few grains of citrate of iron and quinine in their drinking water every other day.

CHAPTER IV

THE MOULTING SEASON

IN the very early days of the Fancy the moulting of birds was generally spoken of as " moulting sickness," which is somewhat of a *misnomer,* as what is a regular, natural process can hardly be called a sickness. Actually, the moult is ordained by Nature to maintain health and full flying efficiency, so that birds can fulfil all their natural functions. And one thing is certain: Unless a Canary moults properly, be it old or young, it cannot be expected to breed with complete success during the following year.

The moulting season has its moments of anxiety. It is during the moult that many a promising youngster is made or marred. The moult finds out the weak spots in a bird's constitution, and causes the development of faults and failings not seen in the first feather.

On the other hand, it must be said that sometimes a bird not thought much of before the moult blossoms out into a winner of firsts, specials and cups owing to the care bestowed upon it, and by the excellent manner in which it comes through its moult.

Some people might compare the casting off of old feathers by birds with the shedding of their foliage by trees. There is some similarity in so far as the shedding process is concerned, but one must remember that a bird, in addition to shedding its old coat, has to grow a new one at the same time, a process which, in trees, is delayed until the springtime.

To understand thoroughly the moulting of a bird one needs to have some knowledge of the structure of feathers. If we take a feather and carefully examine it, we find that it is, roughly speaking, composed of three parts—the quill, the shaft, and the vane, or web. By the former the feather is held to the skin of the bird, the shaft grows out of the quill, running up the centre of the feather, and to the shaft the vane is attached.

The feather grows and is nourished directly from the blood through a small opening at the bottom through which the sustenance for the feather is drawn during the whole time it is growing. This, like the veins of the leaves of a tree, becomes choked in time by the accumulation of the secretions of chemical matter, and the feather, like the leaf, falls away from its support because it is no longer nourished and strengthened.

Truly marvellous is the moulting process when one comes to study it. At this time the Canary, in common with other birds, from the elements contained in its own body, produces the forces which cause its old coat to be cast off and a new one to grow in all its living, glowing pristine beauty.

We are so used to this wonderful process that we never stop to think of its miraculousness. Did we first see a bird moult without knowing anything about it we should be awe-struck, but because we grow up with it, and our eye is trained to it, we fail to pause and think of all that the process means.

When normal conditions prevail, the moult commences by the desiccation of the old feathers; the quills become dull and lifeless, and all the sap is dried out of them. They lose their strength and firmness, the web is bereft of lustre and depth of colour, the quills shrink within their sockets, the surrounding skin becomes shrivelled, and, like the leaves on the trees, they drop off.

Immediately the old feather has dropped out the new begins to fill its place, even if it, like the second tooth of a child, has not already had something to do with the ousting of its forerunner.

It will be obvious to all that the time of the moult must, of necessity, be a time of severe strain on the birds. Not only have they to keep up the natural forces of their body, but they have also to supply from the source of these forces the material, or food, to grow another crop of feathers.

This must naturally have a most exhausting and enervating effect on the internal economy of birds undergoing the process, and thus it becomes our duty to see what we can do to assist our pets to go through the moult with the least amount of discomfort.

First and foremost, we know that warmth is a most desirable and necessary factor in the accomplishment of a quick, healthy, and successful moult. A quick moult is usually a healthy moult, and a healthy moult is, of course, a successful one.

Nature herself has chosen the most fitting time—the end of summer—when the earth is full of heat from the rays of the sun which have been pouring down upon it for some weeks, and which keeps the nights almost as warm as the days. To secure the full benefit of this provision of Nature we want to see to it that the moult in our stock is not delayed. An early moult is a quick one. A late moult is slow, due to unfavourable atmospheric conditions, and very often unforeseen and undesirable complications ensue. Late breeding means late moulting.

Towards the end of June, fanciers should begin to think of putting away all the appurtenances of the breeding season. The sooner breeding is finished the sooner will the old birds drop into moult, that is, the body moult. In this connection it should be noted that the older a Canary becomes, the longer it takes to moult. Thus very old and choice favourites of the stud should be prevented from rearing more than two nests of youngsters, so as to ensure their getting through the moult in a satisfactory manner.

Draught-free Quarters

Warmth being an essential factor in a successful moult, fanciers should see to it that their birds are enabled to get the full benefit of all the warmth which the sun gives, and that they are protected from draughts. Draughts are fatal to Canaries under any circumstances, more especially during the moulting season.

So serious are the effects of a chill caught by exposure to draught during the moult that sometimes the process is stopped altogether, causing the birds unnecessary pain and bringing about illness, possibly death. And even if death does not supervene, the birds are reduced to a poor state of health, never recovering sufficiently from the effects of the bad moult to be ready to take their places in the breeding cages later on.

During the moult birds are, of course, more or less without their full complement of clothes, and thus are very liable to become easily chilled. Therefore, it is the more necessary at this time to exercise the greatest care in their management.

Warmth is better supplied inwardly than outwardly. Good, nourishing, flesh-forming food should be given. A bird to moult well wants to be a little bit above itself, so to speak. A plump, fleshy bird should moult better than a thin one, because it has a greater reserve of stamina to withstand the strain of performing the double function of keeping life going and growing a new coat.

In the early days of the Canary Fancy, many were the substances used to influence colour, and it was a long, long time before fanciers stumbled on to the present system of feeding on tasteless pepper. To-day, when conditions are normal, good colour-foods are to be found on every hand, and also some worthless ones. My advice to breeders is that they should buy, whenever possible, the pure, natural, unadulterated article, be it hot or tasteless, and do the mixing themselves.

One thing to be remembered is that colour-food which looks the deepest in colour is not always the best. Brightness and cleanliness are more important than mere depth of colour, which is often artificially produced by the mixing of oil, sugar, and even dye. A clammy, sticky appearance about a sample of pepper generally denotes the presence of foreign ingredients.

Many think that if a sample of pepper stains everything with which it comes in contact it is all right. This is a mistake. It more generally means that it has been doctored. A little oil mixed with the pepper, either hot or cold, will soon set the colour free.

During the moult, the food must be of a nourishing and generous nature. The egg-food and canary seed should be supplemented with niger, maw and hemp, all of which may be given occasionally, say, a little of one to-day and of another to-morrow, ringing the changes on the three. All these seeds being of an oily nature have a soothing and beneficial effect upon the bird's system at this time of extra strain and stress. These seeds are also useful in tightening the coat, and putting a nice sleek gloss upon it.

Shredded suet (when procurable) and boiled carrot are, again, most useful in this direction, the birds being very fond of both. A little cod-liver oil mixed with the egg-food during the moult will be found to maintain vigour in a high degree.

Some fanciers object to the use of green food during the moult. In my opinion, there is no season of the year when it is more useful. When birds are being colour-fed a quantity of material is being put into their insides which is not in the least nourishing; quite the reverse, in fact. Its tendency is to clog the liver and impede its regular working. Green food is Nature's own corrective for disturbances of the liver, and, therefore, it seems to me to be perfectly reasonable to assume that birds need green food during the moult. I have always made a practice of giving it to them regularly during this trying period, just a sprig a day.

When a bird is falling into moult it appears drowsy and listless. A few days after the feathers will begin to " break," that is, two narrow strips of feathers of a deeper and brighter colour than the old ones will make their appearance on each side of the chest.

The brighter these become, and the more quickly they spread and grow, the greater chance there is of the moult being brought to a successful issue. If the feathers grow slowly it is a sign of weakness and ill-health, and the bird will not look much the better for getting its new coat.

As already mentioned, draughts must be kept away from the birds at this time, or much evil will result. Fresh air is needful, and plenty of it, but no draughts. The bath should be given on every fine day; it is most beneficial in assisting the growth of the new feathers. A tonic is of service during the moult, and every other day a little sulphate of iron, a piece about as big as a pea, should be placed in the drinking water. Should there be signs of constipation, a pinch of magnesia may be placed in the egg-food, or ten drops of glycerine in the drinking water for a day or two.

Avoid Moving Moulters

An equable temperature is essential to a successful moult, therefore birds should not be moved from one room to another during its progress. A successful moult means more than success in the show hall; it means a good breeding season. Birds that moult badly are of little use as breeding stock—a statement which cannot be repeated too often.

The age at which young Canaries moult varies considerably. Youngsters hatched at the end of May often commence to moult before those born in April. Speaking generally, the early hatched birds start when about ten or twelve weeks old, the later ones at about eight weeks.

The symptoms of the moult are unmistakable. The birds go moping about the cage seeking something they cannot find, and instead of hopping about brightly are often found asleep. When this is seen, you may be certain the birds are about to shed their feathers. The colour-food should be given a week or ten days before the birds are expected to start moulting.

Only a small quantity must be given at first, so as to get the birds accustomed to it by degrees. It should be gradually increased until the full strength is used, which should be when the feathers begin to fall. The change needs to be gradual, so as not to upset the birds' digestive organs, as anything which impedes or interferes with the digestion during the moult means that the new coat will look patchy.

As I have previously said, I am no believer in late breeding. If late breeding is indulged in, the old birds can neither be moulted through in the necessary good form, nor in time for the early shows. They should have a week or two in the flights after they have finished rearing, so as to recuperate. While in the flights, and even before their feathers begin to drop, they should be given a little colour-food in their egg-food every day. Immediately the feathers begin to fall they must be put upon the full allowance of colour-food.

Years ago, when depth of colour was more greatly needed than in these latter days, most fanciers used hot pepper only, while others used the following: 4-lb. tasteless pepper; 1-lb. hot Natal pepper; 8-oz. olive oil. Some used to mix sugar with this feed, but I never did, nor do I think it advisable, as a certain amount of fermentation is apt to take place when the sugar is added. A better plan is to mix the sugar in with the colour- and egg-food, as required.

Thus, when mixing, the proportions should be one teaspoonful each of sugar and colour-food to six of egg-food. This should be the limit when the birds are full in the moult. It should be reached gradually from the time the birds are put on colour-food, and be as gradually decreased as the end of the moult approaches, so as to avoid the head and shoulders being too hot in colour.

When the birds are approaching the end of the moult, mix a little freshly ground linseed with the colour-food, not a lot, say, about one teaspoonful to a dozen teaspoonfuls of egg-food. Twice or thrice a week place a slice of raw carrot between the wires of the cage. These two things will greatly assist in adding a gloss, and in tightening up the feathers.

A healthy moult depends to some extent on the conditions under which the birds are moulted. The practice which used to obtain among some fanciers of moulting birds practically in the dark cannot be too strongly condemned. It is both inhumane and unnecessary, as is also the practice of taking away the seed-box when colour-feeding. It is advisable to break the light so as not to have the full glare on the birds at this time; but there is a vast difference between shading the light and having birds practically in the dark.

In the one case the birds will exercise themselves freely, while in the other they are practically still all the time. And there is no doubt that a bird getting natural exercise will moult out more healthily than one not getting adequate exercise. Again, you must not lose sight of the fact that a healthy moult is a good moult, good for colour, and good for stamina, and you want both in the keen competition of the present day.

I advise the use both of green food and an iron tonic during the moult. To obtain the best results in colour-feeding, the liver must be kept working, otherwise half the value of the colour-food is lost. Iron in some form or other is of great benefit during this period.

Its chief purpose is not, as many think, to tighten the feathers at the end of the moult, but to enrich the blood, tone the system, aid in the deposition of colour in the plumage, and also to correct the tendency to laxativeness in the bowels which is often present during the time of colour-feeding.

A little citrate of iron or sulphate of iron given in the drinking water three times a week is most beneficial. In cases of slow moulting a pinch of flowers of sulphur mixed with the food once a day often acts in a manner most advantageous.

Let me repeat, I am no believer in covering the birds up during the moult so that they are in darkness. Light is needful to health, and light the birds must have if they are to come through the moult strong and robust. What, however, is needed is to prevent the sun's rays from having direct access to them.

This can be achieved by hanging a thin muslin covering over the window which will counteract any possible bleaching effect of the sun, while the birds' cages may be covered with a sheet of very thin calico or muslin of just sufficient stoutness to keep the plumage from being soiled.

CHAPTER V

EXHIBITING

HAVING successfully overcome the difficulties of the breeding and moulting seasons, the young fancier often runs up against difficulties when he decides to blossom out as an exhibitor. He has managed to breed and moult some good birds, but he feels diffident about sending them out, chiefly because he does not understand the art of getting stock into show condition.

Show birds need to be kept singly, so as to avoid injury to their plumage, and it is best to keep them in box cages about fifteen or eighteen inches long. In such cages they may be kept clean and quiet. It is quite impossible to have birds in good exhibition form unless they are so kept.

Fanciers who are short of room may use breeding cages for this purpose, giving them a thorough cleansing before placing the birds in them for the winter.

Before the show season starts, and while the birds are still in the moult, all show cases and cages should be overhauled, damaged wires replaced, new paint applied inside and out, broken straps and buckles repaired; in fact, everything put in order for the time when they will be needed.

Having decided to tempt Fate on the show bench, the fancier should send for a schedule to the secretary of one of the shows advertised in CAGE BIRDS. Having received it, he should study the classification carefully and enter the birds in the classes provided for them, returning the entry form to the secretary of the show in good time. On no account be one of those who add so enormously to the work of secretaries by sending *late* entries. Fill up the form clearly and distinctly, and before sending it off check it by the schedule.

A few days before the show you will receive small labels for each of your cages, and a large one for the travelling case. On the latter you must write your name and address for the return journey, and fix it securely to the outside of the case. The small labels must be tied or stuck on the cages of the birds for which they are intended.

The bottoms of the cages should be strewn with seed sufficient to last the birds until their return from the show. Never put bran, sawdust or anything else on the cage bottom. It is not needed, is not in any way beneficial to the birds, and sometimes it leads to unpleasant remarks.

Washing Canaries is a trying business for the beginner. I well remember what a mess I made of the job when attempting it for the first time. More can be learnt from one practical demonstration than by reading a hundred treatises on the subject.

Those who are acquainted with an experienced fancier should make every effort to witness a washing demonstration carried out by him. There is not room in this work for a full exposition of the art of washing, and in any case it is extremely difficult to describe the process satisfactorily in words.

Birds, if they are to be kept in tip-top show condition, require to be fed liberally and well. Travelling to and from shows, hand-washing and the excitement of the showrooms puts a considerable strain upon the nervous system. The best seed only should be used. Canary should be their staple diet, with a little egg-food daily, and a small quantity of maw, rape, or niger by way of variety twice or thrice a week.

If any bird is at all run down a few drops of cod-liver

The proper way to hold a Canary when giving it a hand-wash. Utensils necessary for this job are three bowls, a sponge, soap flakes, a shaving brush, and a soft towel. Before attempting to wash a bird, the novice should witness a practical demonstration by a fellow member of his local cage-bird society.

oil mixed with the egg-food will tone it up. There is much art in keeping birds in show condition. Different birds require different treatment. Experience teaches when and how to give it.

The day before the show, the birds should be run into clean show cages, then each cage should be carefully placed in the travelling case with paper packing to prevent them moving about during transit. Fasten the case securely, and see that the labels are fast. Get your birds off in good time. Do not leave them till the last train or they may be delayed and arrive " too late for competition."

Whenever possible, young fanciers should attend the shows at which they exhibit, for by so doing they will pick up many a good wrinkle and learn much that will help them to ride on the flood-tide of success.

CHAPTER VI

FORMING A STUD

TO establish a strain of birds which will be able to hold its own in the keenest competition is something to tax the energies and skill of the most practical and enthusiastic of fanciers. Fortunately, in these enlightened days the general idea as to what constitutes a good Norwich Plainhead is more widely understood than in years gone by, when one found a certain type of bird winning in the North and another type in the South. Colour and size, as opposed to type, at one time ruled the roost.

To-day all Norwich breeders are agreed that type should be the first consideration. As showing the wonderful unanimity which exists on the subject, I need but quote the fact that the Standard of Excellence drawn up by the Scottish Norwich Plainhead Club was unanimously, and without criticism, adopted by the Southern Norwich Plainhead Canary Club.

There is one thing our brethren across the Border must be congratulated upon, and that is their strong adherence to type. Colour they value, and I have seen some hot ones come out of Aberdeen, but type has ever been their sheet anchor.

What I have written here refers to the standard and ideals issued by the clubs. I wish I could say that all our judges were agreed as to the interpretation of the standard. The majority still seem inclined to favour

49

birds that are big and coarse, and which do not possess that silkiness of feather which denotes quality.

Now, what constitutes an ideal Norwich Plainhead? This is a most important question, and I cannot answer it better than by giving the Standard of Excellence to which I have just referred: —

STANDARD OF EXCELLENCE

COLOUR: Deep, bright, rich, pure and level throughout. SHAPE—Head: Round, full and neat. Neck: Short and thick. Body: Short and chubby, with wide back well filled in. Chest: Deep, broad and full. FEATHER: Soft and silky, with brilliancy and compactness. WINGS AND TAIL: Short, compact, with good carriage. SIZE: Well proportioned. BEAK: Short and stout (clear). LEGS: Well set back (also clear). FEET: Perfect. CONDITION: Health, cleanliness and sound feather. Streaked beak and marked legs not to be a disqualification, but count against the bird to its extent.

SCALE OF POINTS FOR JUDGING

Type	...	...	...	...	...	25
Head	...	...	...	...	...	10
Neck	...	...	...	...	...	10
Wings	...	...	...	...	...	10
Tail	...	...	...	...	...	5
Legs and Feet	...	...	...	...	...	5
Condition	...	...	...	...	...	10
Quality of Feather	...	...	...	...	10
Colour	...	...	...	...	...	10
Staging	...	...	...	...	...	5

(Ideal length 6 to 6¼ inches)   100

This standard provides the universally accepted modern ideal. It reads well on paper, and may seem easy of attainment, but it is not by any means so easy as it looks. Some men who have striven for years have never come within appreciable distance of the standard. But the fault generally has been that they

HEAD: ROUND, FULL & NEAT

EYE: BOLD & UNOBSCURED

NECK: SHORT & THICK

BODY: SHORT & CHUBBY

BACK: WELL FILLED IN

WINGS & TAIL: SHORT, COMPACT & WELL CARRIED

BEAK: SHORT & STOUT

FRONT: DEEP, BROAD & FULL

LEGS: WELL SET BACK

LENGTH: NOT TO EXCEED 6½"

Features in a model show specimen

have not proved thorough enough in their methods.

In starting out to reach the ideal, the young fancier should first of all sit down and count the cost. Not the cost in coin only, but the cost of labour and of time. The ideal cannot be reached in a season or two; in fact, it is practically impossible of attainment. A *perfect* Norwich Canary has never yet been bred.

To the true fancier, breeding is the most enjoyable and interesting branch of his hobby. Weeks will be spent working out the different matings of his stock according as experience prompts him. Sometimes his schemes are " all trumps," at others he misses every trick. Fortunately the latter is not often the case, but when it is so it proves how hard a battle we have to fight with the natural laws of reversion in the animal world.

When everything in the bird-room is prepared for their reception, one must set about acquiring the birds. How are they to be obtained, and from whom? The best plan is to go to some reliable fancier, noted as a *breeder* of high-class exhibition stock, and ask him to do his best for you. Describe your needs, and tell him the state of your exchequer. Speaking generally, you will not regret trusting yourself to the honour of such a man.

Few and Good

When purchasing, it is well to remember that the best are the cheapest in the end, so invest what money you can spare in two pairs of good birds rather than half a dozen mediocre pairs. Young fanciers often make the mistake of preferring quantity to quality, thinking that out of a multitude of young they are more likely to breed a winner or two. This is a mistake. Like produces like, and if you want to breed exhibition specimens you must have good-face-value birds as foundation stock.

It is not, however, altogether necessary that stock birds should be show birds. As a matter of fact, most of the Plainheads which have distinguished themselves in the past on the show bench were not bred from winners, but from the brothers and sisters, uncles and aunts, and other close relations of famous birds.

From this it must not be inferred that tip-top exhibition specimens are of little use as stock birds. Quite the reverse, and when all the circumstances are favourable I prefer show birds for stock purposes. The reason why some exhibition birds do not prove good stock birds is often due to the fact that they are exhibited too often during the season.

The excitement of being on the benches has some slight effect on their nervous systems, but it must be said that many exhibitors maintain that their birds seem to enjoy outings to shows, and that breeding vigour is in no way impaired by such activities.

If the original stock is purchased in the manner I advise, the owner is saved a lot of worry and anxiety in selecting birds that may suit each other. Further, no matter how much care is exercised in selecting birds, if they come from different studs they are not likely to breed youngsters as good as themselves, whereas if chosen from one stud they are almost certain to " hit " and breed decent stock the first season.

The great secret of success in breeding livestock is in keeping the blood running in family lines. The breeder who goes here, there and everywhere for stock retards his progress instead of advancing it.

There is a great deal of skill needed when it comes to mating Norwich and other Canaries, far more, indeed, than the novice might suppose. We want to so pair them that the good and bad points of each partner are counterbalanced as far as possible, and made to blend into one perfect whole. This is not to be accomplished in a season or two. Slow and sure must be the motto.

Mating birds successfully is the outcome of years of experience. The most successful breeders are those who mate their birds to produce results which practice has told them they may expect. They breed for desirable characteristics and get them. They weigh up all the good and bad points, and then pair their stock so as to get the maximum of the good and the minimum of the bad. They do not always get what they seek, because Nature has a little trick of putting a spoke in the wheel and causing the birds to " throw back."

Although the power of reversion is strong, it must not be forgotten that like produces like when a certain line of breeding is followed year after year. It often happens that birds of dissimilar character are matched together to produce ideal specimens. This is because the breeder knows their ancestry thoroughly. Otherwise it could not be done.

In a general manner the cock bird influences colour, feather, and size, while the hen is largely responsible for shape and constitution in her progeny. Like every rule, this has its exceptions, owing to the special prepotency of one of a given pair. Some birds mark their progeny with personal features that seem fixed in the blood so strongly as to overcome all opposing factors.

Sometimes a bird will pass on certain characteristics that are not visible in its parents, properties which you will have to go back two, three, or even four or more generations to find.

It is not wise to put together birds possessing the same faults. Of course, there are occasions when it is not needful to stick rigidly to this rule, but as a general principle it is a good one to work on. As an example, two birds failing in carriage or colour should never be paired together, yet if they are both bred from birds which excel in these properties, or from a strain excelling in such, it would not matter.

If I were asked to select a pair of birds for breeding from among a lot of whose ancestry I knew nothing, I should proceed on the following lines: My shape, style and head I should expect to find in my hen. Colour, feather, and size I should look for in the cock. My reasons for so doing would be that in nine cases out of ten the cock influences the outward characteristics of the progeny, while in like ratio the hen exercises her influence over those points which have mostly to do with the general organization and the properties which are hidden.

The hen has far more to do with shape, or type, than many are willing to believe, but myself, I would rather breed from a bad-shaped or a bad-headed cock than from a hen with these failings. Never, unless absolutely forced to do so, would I breed with a hen that failed in head properties. Quality comes from both sides, but experience teaches me that the hen has the bigger say in the matter. Therefore, although I should select my hen primarily for type, I should like her to possess good quality feather as well.

Although I have described a pair of birds such as I should put together, it must not be forgotten that they may not " hit." One or other of them may be unusually prepotent. If so, the union will not be a happy one as regards quality of offspring. Then the question of relative age is a factor that often upsets a carefully thought out mating. Given two birds in good health, the younger partner will usually have the biggest say in the properties which appear in the progeny.

At times the result seems ruled by the law of averages, and a vigorous yearling throws stock which has nothing in common with a mate several seasons older. Stranger still, some quite aged birds duplicate most excellent properties, even when paired to birds of less merit and age. The most successful matings consist in setting weak points against strong ones, and trying to blend all the good properties in one or more of the progeny.

After a year or two of breeding, a fancier who uses his understanding will know his stock, and can then build it up point by point, each year seeking to improve some particular property. To do this he mates two birds both excelling in some special feature—it may be colour—with the idea of " doubling-up " on that special property. If two good-coloured birds are mated together, it stands to reason that they are far more likely to throw good-coloured young than if one of them is of bad colour. In the same way feather, carriage, shape, or markings may be improved.

All-round excellence is what is desired in the high-class exhibition Norwich Plainhead. This can best be attained by building up the fabric bit by bit, here a little and there a little. It is impossible to get all the desired properties at once, and he who expects to do so will meet with nothing but failure and disappointment.

The expert breeder working on scientific lines seeks to improve his stock year by year in some particular point, and he goes on in this way each season until he at last possesses birds which can hold their own with the best in the Fancy.

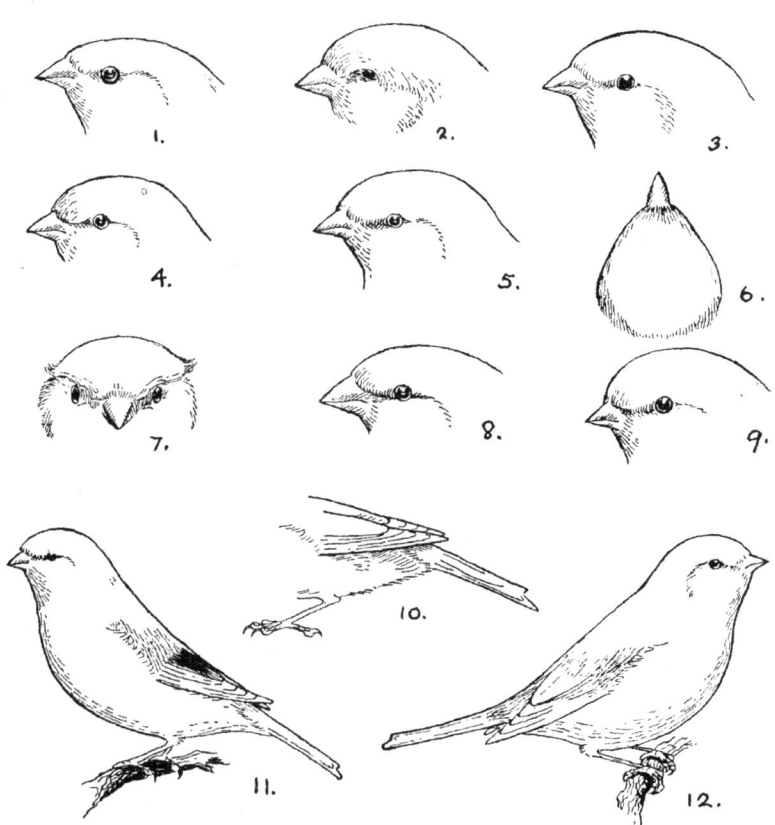

Variations in Norwich : (1) Flat head ; (2) Browiness ; (3) No cheeks ; (4) Poor back-skull ; (5) Long head ; (6) Pinched entrance ; (7) Showing "horns " ; (8) Coarse beak ; (9) Good head ; (10) Hinged tail ; (11) Duck-backed ; (12) Robin-tailed.

My experience is that you cannot bring a stud to a high degree of excellence so quickly if you try to do it all at once, as you can if you make slow and sure progress by effecting improvement by degrees, and this I know is also the experience of leading breeders in all kinds of live stock.

Although I have mentioned the properties I should look for in the cock and hen in a good pair intended for stock, do not let me be misunderstood. I do not decry breeding with exhibition specimens; on the contrary I believe in breeding from the very best when and wherever possible, and in such cases the nearer the birds come to the ideal, the better I am pleased.

If in his first season the beginner has managed to breed a few nice youngsters, he should, if possible, ask the advice of the breeder from whom he bought his stock as to their mating for the second season.

If he cannot obtain such help, and the parents have been unrelated, he should breed some of the young back to their sire and dam. This in-breeding, some people argue, is unnatural. They say it weakens the constitution, brings about disease, and is the forerunner of all ills. I do not subscribe to such views.

In-breeding, properly carried out, is not only quite correct and proper, but it also leads to success. Its abuse, however, can bring about trouble in every shape and form. Not carried too far, it must be conducted on careful, methodical lines with patience and watchfulness. In-breeding (line-breeding) is, in my view, the only sure way in which to produce Plainheads and other Canaries which can win consistently season after season at the leading exhibitions.

Some fanciers are so constituted that they must carry everything to excess; the happy medium has no place in their thoughts or actions. In their hands, in-breeding would soon result in a diminution of standard properties, and in a few years their studs, after manifesting a marked tendency to contract all sorts of disease, would gradually decrease and dwindle away from sheer lack of stamina.

Guided by the description of my ideal, the young fancier should have no difficulty in mating up his stock the second year, even if he is unable to secure the assistance of some more experienced fancier.

Doubling-up on Good Points

If the old, original hen is of the correct shape and size, short and cobby in body and short in feather, also possessing plenty of quality and good colour, she should be paired to the one particular son most like his father, and the old sire should be mated to his daughter which is most like her mother. Such mating as this is, so to speak, rolling all the good points of your original stock together. One of the most successful Norwich breeders I know swears by this sort of mating in the second year, while another has repeatedly told me that all his best show examples have been bred from brothers and sisters. I have bred both ways, and have met with success from each kind of pairing.

It sometimes happens that a fancier puts together two birds which excel in a certain feature, yet not one of their progeny is beyond mediocrity, so far as that particular property is concerned. This often proves a stumbling-block to the novice, as he has imagined that two birds extra good in one point would produce youngsters excelling in that respect.

He finds it is not so, and in his disappointment he discards both old and young and starts afresh. Foolish fellow! he is throwing away birds of untold value. The point sought for must have been in those young birds, which another season would most likely reveal.

An experienced breeder knows this, and he would pair sire to daughter and dam to son, the rest brother to sister, and find the next season's results approach the desire of his heart. It is in matters such as this where long experience often keeps a fancier from making a false step.

Of course, this close pairing of relations, irrespective of everything else, must not be continued indefinitely or disaster swift and sure will overtake the stud in which it is perpetrated. All the time a close watch must be kept for any falling off in fecundity and stamina.

If the original foundation birds have been purchased as I recommend, they will be related in some degree, and if my system of mating is followed in the second season, the third season will find the fancier with sufficient experience to know how to manage subsequent pairings, and also with birds suitable for his purpose.

Before I leave this question of forming a stud, or strain, I would strongly urge upon my readers the necessity of keeping their best hens. Some breeders think more of their cocks than their hens. This is a mistake.

If I had to decide between a pair in which the cock was a first-class one and the hen a second-rater, and one in which the cock was a stock bird and the hen a champion, I should go for the latter. Good hens have far more to do with the success of a strain than good cocks. Type comes from the hens, and a man who is constantly changing his hens will never fix good type in his stud.

We want our birds to be of uniform type, and that type the one which most nearly approaches to the description of an ideal bird, as set out in the standard of excellence. Individual excellence and ancestry are the two most important considerations in breeding stock.

Individual merit alone cannot be relied upon always, for from birds almost approaching standard requirements we must inevitably get some very poor specimens. A chance good bird with poor breeding factors in his make-up should never be used. On the other hand, a bird of good breeding whose lineage will bear looking into will, in most cases, prove a valuable breeder, even though not particularly impressive in appearance.

All fanciers should keep a faithful record of the pedigrees of their entire stock, and thus be at all times able to tell if any one particular bird is related, and if so, how closely to the one with which it is desired to mate it. CAGE BIRDS Breeding Register enables a breeder to keep his stock under complete, intelligent control. It helps him in his efforts to avoid too close in-breeding, or to go too far outside a certain line when wanting a mate for any particular bird.

In concluding this chapter, let me once again impress upon all Norwich fanciers never to part with their best hens, and to keep a faithful record of all breeding performances and pedigrees. If you act upon these lines, you will, in a few years, establish a strain that will bring you not only fame and pleasure, but also some considerable pecuniary reward.

Adopt a first-rate system of close pedigree breeding. After a few seasons—assuming that you started with the right kind of stock—you will produce extra fine show specimens and be able to command satisfactory prices for those youngsters which you have for disposal.

CHAPTER VII

PRODUCING THE IDEAL

IN the foregoing chapters I have dealt more or less with Canary breeding generally, much of what I have written being just as applicable to one variety of Canary as another. This chapter, however, will deal with the Norwich Plainhead in particular.

In it I shall endeavour to describe the ideal Norwich, not in the technical language of the standard, but in my own phraseology I shall describe in detail how that ideal is to be produced, starting with the head.

The head of an ideal Norwich should be very thick and chubby, presenting an appearance of roundness even though it be not round. There must be no flatness about either front, top, sides, or back. It should rise gracefully from the base of the beak, and fall away into the neck at its junction with the base of the skull.

The face should also be chubby; hollow or flat cheeks are altogether wrong in an up-to-date Norwich Plainhead. Viewed from the front, back, or in profile, the head should have the appearance of roundness; there must be no angularity anywhere, no flatness of skull, and no overhanging eyebrows.

The eye should be bold and set in a line with the beak. It should be nearly in the centre of the head, though not quite central, or the bird will look too marble-headed, and that is undesirable. The eye should be set a trifle nearer to the beak than to the back of the skull. The beak must be short and neat, neither too fine nor too stout. Any suggestion of coarseness is a failing.

A beak which is too fine gives the bird a mean appearance, and one that is too stout spoils the beautiful outline of the skull when viewed in profile. But, still worse, it is often accompanied by flatness of skull and overhanging brows.

A typical Norwich should be short, thick and stout in neck—in a word, bull-necked. It can hardly be too thick or too short. Many otherwise good birds are spoilt by having longish, thin necks. This failing is usually seen in yellows of high colour and quality; they are very apt to run off fine in neck.

The head, neck and shoulders of a good Norwich should be bunched up together. The neck should be just sufficient to show that there is something between the head and the shoulders. To resurrect a paradox I once heard expressed by an old breeder: " A good-necked Norwich should have no neck." Visualize a Bullfinch if you want to gain a good idea of what a first-rate Plainhead's neck should be like.

The body must be round and compact, deep through from back to breast, broad in the chest and shoulders, well rounded in front and at the sides, while the back itself should be broad and slightly rounded. A flat back is wrong, so also is what is known as a roached back. The roundness of the back should be almost imperceptible, and rise from the sides and not from the shoulders.

From the shoulders to the tail the back should present an appearance not of flatness, nor of roundness, but of being well filled in. While the front of the body, or chest, requires to be bold, deep, and broad, that portion behind the legs should be altogether different.

Behind the legs there should be little body, and what there is should have a " well cut away " appearance. The ideal Norwich is short all over. Many of the big ones are far from being really compact in shape. They have breadth and depth it is true, but they have far too much length.

The wings should be well set into the shoulders; they should also be short, tightly braced, and carried very close to the body. The flights must lie nice and evenly, with the tips meeting just over the root of the tail. This is where many good birds fall short. Their wings, instead of meeting and being well balanced, cross each other.

This arises very often through the back being narrow and roached, and sometimes by the birds being flat-sided. The wings should rest upon the root of the tail, and not be cocked up so that daylight may be seen between them and the finish of the back. Bad wing carriage is a rather prevalent fault in some exhibition Norwich at the present time.

The tail needs to be short, very tightly folded, and carried at a nice angle from the body, of which it should very definitely present the appearance of being a part. Some tails look as though they do not belong to the body that carries them, but have been stuck into the trunk because a caudal appendage appears necessary to the bird. Some are too long, some too wide, and some seem to work on a hinge, and not in unison with the body. A well-made tail adds greatly to the finish of a bird.

It matters not how well built the body of a Norwich may be if it is not coupled with good carriage. The best body ever seen may be spoilt by bad carriage, even as a moderate-bodied bird may show a great advantage by reason of its possessing correct carriage.

A Norwich should be smart and lively in its movements, and show a reasonable jauntiness and pertness of carriage. In this connection mention should be made of the legs; they have much to do with correct carriage of the body.

If the legs are too long the body will be carried too upright and not enough across the perch. On the other hand, if they are too short the bird will look cloddy and heavy, and be somewhat sluggish in its movements.

With legs of medium length, the bird is able to put just sufficient boldness into its carriage to throw its chest well across the perch, and for its head to be lifted well up in a bold, fearless manner. So much for structural properties. We now come to those which are really the finishing points.

Having a body approaching the ideal, we want it clothed in a coat of soft, silky feather, the under flue of which should be as soft and yielding as floss silk, while the top should be firm, bright and glistening, like a piece of highly finished dress silk. Anything approaching a harsh, dry, cottony appearance is altogether out of place in an exhibition Norwich.

Colour is all that is now needed to make the bird I have depicted a veritable champion. Colour, as mentioned earlier, was at one time the alpha and omega of a Norwich Plainhead. It is not so to-day, but even yet it plays a great part in judges' decisions, and always will, because nothing attracts the eye so much as rich colour.

To meet the keenness of present-day competition, a winning Norwich needs to be one rich golden-orange tinge right through. This must be both bred and fed for. With colour-feeding I have already dealt in the chapter on " Moulting "; of the former more hereafter.

Correct Type All-important

Type is the first thing to be thought of in connection with breeding exhibition Norwich, for it is type or shape which makes the difference between one breed of Canary and another. I have fully described what the ideal bird should be, and the best way to perpetuate that ideal is to breed with birds which approximate thereto.

This, however, is difficult in many cases, but I would urge upon all breeders that if they want to strengthen and improve their studs, both parents must be birds of type.

As it is not possible at all times for the breeder to mate birds which approach the ideal, I will describe how he should proceed with those which are more or less faulty in the principal points, and, while not fit for show, may, nevertheless, by the excellency of other properties, and by virtue of their good pedigree, make most valuable stock birds.

From what I have said in the chapter on " Forming a Stud," my readers will have gathered that I attach extreme importance to the hens. Whatever faults the cocks may possess, I like the hens to be as near perfection as possible, especially when breeding for improved type.

Strong, heavy cock birds which may, perhaps, be a trifle too long in body or too coarse in feather, make splendid mates for those neat, short, chubby, high-quality hens which just fail a trifle in size for exhibition purposes.

A hen is none the worse for being a trifle undersized, provided she has all the other necessary qualifications; in fact, such a hen is far to be preferred to a large, coarse hen.

Large hens are not, as a rule, good mothers. Moreover, they breed youngsters which are ungainly and clumsy in carriage, and, generally speaking, their progeny lack quality. The neat, natty little hen, if of good type, is the ideal hen for stud purposes.

As type comes in great measure from the hens, the man who would be successful and make a name for himself as an exhibitor and breeder, must study very carefully the upkeep of a good stud of hens. This can only be done by refraining from breeding with hens which are narrow in head or body, those which are lacking in depth and width, those which are hard and harsh in feather, or hens which are clumsy and awkward in gait.

Unless a strain is carefully watched, deterioration in size will set in, and the way to avoid this is to keep away from cocks which, although they may be brimful of colour and quality, are just a bit fine and whippety in body. Such birds are nice to look at, but they are not much use as founders of a strain of birds which are likely to win prizes.

Quality of feather is a property which we all admire, for no matter how good a bird may be in type, colour, and style, if it has not quality it does not completely satisfy a breeder or a judge. Years ago, when I first engaged in the Norwich Fancy, quality used to be kept up by mating a Lizard and a Norwich together every now and then, and it was not at all unusual to find what was called " a dapple backed 'un " among the birds shown in the unevenly marked, or, as it was then more generally termed, the variegated class. And very handsome birds they were, too.

The Lizard cross used to give a beautiful softness and silkiness of feather which was most enchanting, while at the same time it added a rich metallic lustre to the colour. I have often said, when lecturing on Norwich Plainheads, that if breeders of to-day would, now and again, take a dip into Lizard blood, it would pay them. It might mean a temporary sacrifice of size, but that could be rectified fairly quickly.

The way I should recommend the cross to be used would be by mating a rich-coloured, chubby, fine-feathered buff Norwich hen to a silver Lizard cock. If it was carried out on these lines there would not be much loss of size. Young *cocks* bred from this cross should not be used for breeding, but sold as songsters. If they should be used they would tend to lower the size of the strain. Only the hens should be employed, and these should be paired to Norwich cocks excelling in size.

If it is not thought advisable to dip into Lizard blood, then recourse must be had to green blood, and here let me say that the man who seeks to build up a winning strain of Norwich ought always to have in his breeding-room a large percentage of birds showing green feathering, ranging from ticked and lightly marked specimens to heavily marked or nearly green birds.

The clear bird is considered to be the highest form of the breeder's art, because it is farthest away from the original wild Canary, but the constant pairing of birds that are clear or lightly ticked often leads to a loss of quality. Therefore, it is needful to keep a tight hand on one's breeding stock in this respect. If clear hens are used, then the cocks should be more or less marked, and *vice versa*.

This system of breeding is followed by our most successful fanciers, and that fact alone is its best recommendation. One important advantage attaching to the use of green blood is that not only does it add to the quality of the birds, but it also improves colour and increases the stamina of a strain.

That is where the old-time breeders of Nottingham, Northampton, Leicester, Plymouth, Norwich and elsewhere, used to excel. They bred for colour. They knew the value of employing variegated birds to enhance both quality of feather and colour, and they always used them in the production of their clears and ticks.

Colour being such an important factor in the awards of the judges, it behoves the breeder to pay much attention to its production. Some breeders foolishly argue that as colour may be put in through the medium of colour-food during the moult, there is no need to breed for it. This is a great fallacy, as the birds which are bred for colour take colour-food more readily than those which are not so bred.

Further, a bird which has a good store of natural colour does not require so great an intake of colour-food as does one in which breeding for colour has not been considered. Yellow variegated cocks are most useful birds for keeping up colour in a stud, but, strange to say, such birds as a general rule fail somewhat in type, being built on rather more racy lines than the clears.

In using such birds in the breeding-room they must be paired to buff hens which are of fair size, though not in the least clumsy. Buff-marked birds, on the other hand, are often very thick and chubby, therefore they can be used freely with yellow hens, either clear or lightly marked.

Buff-marked cocks mated with yellow, lightly marked hens often throw most magnificent birds so far as colour and quality are concerned, and without any great loss of type or size. But colour alone considered, and for improving colour in a strain, I prefer yellow-marked cocks and lightly marked buff hens.

Some men are so mentally constituted that they cannot work on orthodox lines. They must always be doing something which is out of the general run of things. To such men do we owe much of the progress which the world has made.

The accepted method of pairing Plainheads and other Canaries is yellow to buff, or buff to yellow, yet some breeders double-yellow and double-buff; that is, pair two yellows or two buffs together. This is done in the one case with the idea of improving colour, and in the other of gaining increased size.

Now, each of such crossings or matings is attended with great risks. In double-yellowing the progeny usually lose substance of body and strength of feather, while in double-buffing there is generally a loss of quality. Personally, I do not favour the doubling process. Colour can always be increased by the methods

I have already pointed out, and size also can be maintained by judicious selection of cock birds possessing size and a fair amount of green blood.

These off-the-line systems of breeding are all very well for old, experienced breeders who understand their stock thoroughly, and who, when they break away from orthodox methods, have a definite aim and object in view. So far as double-buffing is concerned, I consider it the less disastrous of the two doubles in its effects. Its worst result, as a rule, is to make feathering more coarse.

Although I do not consider either doubles are needed if judicious care is exercised in the general matings of a stud, yet I am not so prejudiced against these matings as to say their results always make for harm and not for good. On the contrary, I think there comes from double-buffing a most valuable asset, and that is increased " meal."

In mating two buffs care should be taken that they are what are known as " quality buffs." That is, birds extra fine in feather and very rich in colour. It is rank madness to double-buff with birds that are large and coarse, or that are heavily marked.

What is a ticked bird? This used to be a fairly simple proposition. To-day it is not. We have no definite rule. Some clubs say " a tick is a mark that may be covered by a threepenny-piece," others say a sixpenny-piece.

Many years ago, before the reformer's hand touched our schedules, some of the classes used to read, " Ticked, Marked, or Variegated." In these classes were generally to be found three or four, and sometimes more, evenly marked birds. These used, nine times out of ten, to secure the premier positions, because the judges, knowing the difficulty of producing even-marks, used to make some slight concession as regards type in such birds compared with the ticked or unevenly marked exhibits.

Then for some years the schedules throughout the country read, " Ticked, or Unevenly Marked," which shunted the evenly marked birds to that refuge of the homeless, the A.O.V., where they have had to take pot luck with Belgians, Scots, etc. As a result, the breeding of evenly marked birds has become almost a lost art.

A well-balanced, four-pointed buff Norwich is one of the handsomest birds imaginable, and it has been a matter of deep regret to me to watch the gradual decline in popularity of such a charming fellow. Nowa-days, the general practice is to provide " Lightly Varie-gated " and " Heavily Variegated " classes at the lead-ing exhibitions.

In other branches of the Fancy the chief aim of specialist clubs is to do everything possible to strengthen varieties which are weak. In the Norwich Canary Fancy an opposite policy seems to prevail. The Norwich Plainhead Club has been in existence for many years, but I am not aware of it ever having done anything to encourage the breeding of what all must agree are the most beautiful members of the Norwich family; I refer to the attractive four- and six-pointed birds.

To those who would like to engage in bringing these lost beauties back to their old position in the Fancy, every encouragement should be given. I feel sure the results would well repay them.

They would meet with many disappointments, it is true, yet, on the other hand, the breeding of a really well-marked four- or six-pointed bird would cause them to attain greater fame and notoriety than the breeding of half a dozen first-rate clears.

There are plenty of birds to be obtained to-day that would form the nucleus of a good stud for the breeding of evenly marked birds. Breeders everywhere are paying more attention to the use of green blood, and among their stocks are to be found many birds with markings on the eyes and wings, markings which only want a little careful selection and breeding to make them permanent.

Quite a number of good three-pointed birds are about, that is, birds marked on both wings and one eye, or both eyes and one wing; others may be seen with wing marks only, and some with eye marks only. These birds would prove invaluable to anyone willing to concentrate upon the breeding of even-marks.

A three-pointed cock could be paired with a hen marked on eyes or wings only, or a cock marked on eyes only could be paired with a wing-marked hen, and so on. The great thing to remember in breeding even-marks is to avoid the use of two birds that are heavily marked.

Thus, if a bird with heavy eye and wing markings was used, its mate should have very light eye markings and no wing marking, or light wing markings and no eye marking. A perfectly marked bird should be mated to one lightly marked, and so on.

PART II by A. W. SMITH

CHAPTER I

A FRESH START

THE Norwich Plainhead was the first variety of Canary I took up. That was many years ago. With these birds came my initial experiences, successes and setbacks—my graduation from the novice status. Then came the war, during the course of which my outdoor birdroom was badly damaged, so that I had to get rid of all my stock of various kinds of Canaries.

During 1945, however, I made another start in my repaired bird-house with Norwich Plainheads. Time has shown me again revelling in most other varieties, but there it is, Norwich were installed first.

Come to think of it, this places me in a unique and happy position to discuss Plainheads with those who may also be restarting, or perhaps some have wished to begin with this handsome variety and longed for some lead. Let us get together.

That word " handsome " came spontaneously to me, and truly a good Norwich is a handsome Canary indeed. For myself, I was fortunate in obtaining, during 1945, some very promising new stock. That is all one can reasonably expect. It is not the cream of an established breeder's stock—that would be impossible to secure—but one certainly needs birds that show promise. Norwich breeders, in the main, are a splendid body of fanciers, but, sporting as most of them are, one cannot be so irrational as to expect a start on the same rung of the ladder as themselves.

However, promising Norwich we must have, and can get, but we must be reconciled to the fact that each bird will have its failings as well as the good features that commend it to us. Within the limits of our purse we have to obtain birds with the minimum of the unwanted but with a complete absence of some really undesirable characters, which I shall dwell upon later.

Now, this outlook indicates a small nucleus stock only, and, as you will learn, we shall in the long run make far better progress by starting slowly. The great virtue of a small beginning is that we are able to practise that age-old advice in exhibition breeding—quality before quantity. Good Norwich have always been worth good money, but spend wisely on a choice few.

Arising out of the slogan, "Quality before Quantity," do not be misled into thinking that you cannot expect quantity when breeding with your quality Norwich. Vigorous Norwich Plainheads can be as prolific as any other Canaries. Therefore I do not recommend a novice to buy from stocks which have some " good-lookers " among them, but are of low fecundity. There are such in every variety, and one must avoid them. We do not want glorious Norwich as figments of our imagination, but in flesh and feather.

Mind you, I am not suggesting that you can take up Norwich Plainheads and breed with hundred per cent. results; far from it, for, in common with all varieties, so much depends on method, time, accommodation, individual aptitude, and the unforeseen. It may be said, however, that Norwich can be prolific and self-rearing, and it is, therefore, up to us to purchase only " good doers," as our Scottish friends term vigorous breeding birds.

You may be thinking about the scourge of " lumps," a disease that thinned the ranks of Norwich breeders considerably a few years ago. I had in mind that trouble, too, when buying my new stock, and I recommend purchasers to ask point-blank of sellers: " Is your strain troubled with lumps?" If the answer is evasive, or if it is truthfully stated that lumps are prevalent, then shy off such studs. But if a seller is able to give you a qualified reply, you can buy, fully aware of the possibilities you may have to contend with.

If he says, " absolutely free of the trouble," buy with alacrity, even if his birds are not so good to look upon, perhaps not so big, as those of the previous breeder's. They can be improved upon, if you are fancier enough to strive hard for improvement.

Well now, assuming that we are agreed on the advisability of a slow start. Let us see how I myself have fared. Some of you will think that as a judge I am in a stronger position than many fanciers when it comes to choosing a likely Norwich, and that I am fortunate in knowing all the best Norwich breeders. With these thoughts of yours in mind I propose to explain exactly what happened in my case, and how you should proceed and what you may expect.

As to acquaintance with the best Norwich breeders, you, too, can be on the best of terms with this grand fraternity. They will welcome you to their ranks, if you are, as you ought to be, a good sort, a good sport, a painstaking fancier.

Well, my first acquisitions were three hens, a 1943 variegated yellow, a 1944 wing-marked yellow, and a 1944 heavily variegated buff. Note that the hens come first. Seek the best obtainable, but not at the close of a show season, when even indifferent hens are at a premium. Get them at the *beginning* of the show season, if you possibly can. Established breeders well know that good hens are the keystone of a successful stock. High-grade cocks are far more readily available, even late in the season, and they can come to hand later, as mine did.

Now we will discuss these hens individually. The 1943 yellow was a marvel for type, neat all over and perfectly balanced, but small. Myself, I thought her a little peach, a model; yes, a diminutive edition of the real thing, but too small for most breeders. Inquiry revealed that she had two nests only during 1944. The first was a failure, but she proved a good feeder in the second round. As to her antecedents, I learned that she was exceedingly well bred for three generations, and, of course, she looked it, *while size was present in each generation.*

The 1944 wing-marked yellow was a nice hen, medium to small in size, only fair in head, sound body type, a wee bit wide at root of tail, but of extra good quality feather, with extraordinary depth of natural colour, which at first made me challenge her sex. I examined her in a show cage and found that she had a splendid capacity for showing for all she was worth —a most desirable trait. Many of us have despaired of those Norwich, good in the stock cage but which slump in the show cage. You should appreciate this in your Norwich. Her pedigree was not quite so promising, but decidedly good on her sire's side, and if applied genetics mean anything, she must " click." She is from a free-breeding strain.

The young variegated buff hen excelled in pedigree, some of the best blood in the land flowing in her veins. She was a good all-round hen, not superlative, medium to big in size, certainly as big as I wish in a breeding hen, of very fine quality, only fair colour, with that dull, " mousey " tone of variegation. I cannot depend on her for colour production.

You see, then, these hens, while very desirable, were not winners, and you may not be able to secure birds as good as these. But who knows, you may, perhaps, do better. Experience, however, teaches us that we have to breed the *best* type of hens ourselves, that is, better hens than we can ever hope to purchase.

Now for the yellow cock to mate with the buff hen. I saw many very likeable yellows, and tentatively I enquired about quite a number of really good potential mates. In fairness to their owners, I must say they were all ready to help me. Finally, the best of them all came my way, a 1944 variegated yellow, and he was also the smallest. " I cannot understand it," said his previous owner, " when one notes the size of his father and of his brother."

As I saw this bird for the first time, he struck me as being a neat model. He improved a little in girth as he grew older, with not a corner or hollow anywhere, wings beautifully braced, tail narrow and piped, head classically moulded and carried. The buff hen was sizeable, and this small cock has big forebears on both sides of his parentage. He may be able to produce youngsters bigger than himself; indeed, he should do so.

All this time I was also on the lookout for a suitable buff cock for the two yellow hens. I saw several superior specimens that were for sale, and some that were not, of course, but the response to my enquiries at least assured me that I could get a good one.

Before deciding definitely, I wrote to another of my distant Norwich friends, asking if he could let me have a good-headed cock, no matter what age, as long as he was virile. Don't forget, I had two *young* hens. He replied: " I have a 1942 variegated buff cock which I think you will like, one of a nest of five, and he bred five very nice youngsters last year."

" One that I would like! "—no superlatives—sounded real good to me, so I asked him to send it on. When I saw this buff cock I knew my search was ended. He possessed a bold round head, not inordinately big, full short neck, short firm flights, and these in his third year; tightly packed, rigid tail, full round front, firm close feather, clean cutaway, and obviously in fine fettle.

His faults were minor ones, in view of the hens I possessed. Short as were his wings, he clipped them slightly which betokened that his shoulders were not quite proportionately wide in relation to his general rotundity. As for size, he had plenty, in girth, not length—a stock bird supreme.

A lesson arises here. Good stock birds are not merely outsize specimens, whose only recommendation is bulk. The desirable attributes must be embodied in them, but if accompanied by a measure of size, so much the better.

Now let us sum up what I had in my new foundation Norwich Plainheads. Quality of feather was apparent in all the birds, a very strong point indeed, and one which I earnestly impress upon newcomers to this

The two admirable specimens here portrayed are (left) a clear yellow hen and an evenly wing-marked buff cock. They excel in every show characteristic.

Fancy. Never sacrifice this paramount feature to any of the crazes that from time to time beset every variety.

Other features are firm flights, rigid tails, clean cutaways, variegation and vigour. The last-named is a prime essential in founding a strain. Slight variations occur in body-structure (none bad, and all generally short in build). As regards heads, those of the cocks satisfied me, and cocks usually transmit this property.

Beaks: One of the yellow hens had this feature a trifle long. Colour: Remember that buff hen. Lastly, size: Two birds were definitely small, one medium to small, and two plenty big enough to please.

You are by now wondering, I suppose, whether I reckon to breed a Norwich like unto the grand picture that figures as a frontispiece to this book. I don't know. I can only hope, and I shall pursue that hope with each breeding season. Shall I breed winners? Maybe I shall, but I am one of those fanciers who realize that others are travelling the same road, with the same splendid objective, and their produce may beat the best of mine. That, however, will only spur me on. It is the chase which is the best part of the hunt.

Small Stud Satisfactory

Of course, I shall build up on my few birds. I shall add to them, and dispose of several. Much will depend on how they breed, the time I can give to them, and certain other considerations.

By now I have laid all my cards on the table, so to speak, and what have you learned? You must be impressed by the fact that, after all, you do not need a big stock involving you in too great an expense, making serious inroads into the seed supply, to venture into this delightful breed. Indeed, the bigger your initial stock, the greater must be the number of birds inferior to your choicest, the more complex your annual selection of breeding stock, to say nothing of increased expense.

Incidentally, that greatly renowned Scottish Plainhead breeder, the late Charles Bryden, the only one to win a National Norwich Trophy outright at three " Palace " Shows, was content with only twelve breeding pairs, and this in his heyday of fame!

Next, you probably feel that I am mighty particular, patient and persevering in my quest for new birds. So must you be. For heaven's sake don't ask, or write to, a successful Norwich breeder for a bird that is the epitome of all the requisite good qualities. You will not, you cannot, get it. He, like myself, has received many such requests, and we say to ourselves: " What a hope these fellows have! We have been striving to produce such a marvellous Norwich ourselves for years."

Perhaps you will think that you are not in such a favoured position as myself in knowing what to accept, what to avoid. That is my real mission in penning these chapters, to equip you with the right Norwich ideals, remembering, however, that experience is really the best teacher.

Experience. Maybe you are a beginner, but do not let that deter you. Set your goal at the top, make up your mind to get there. Most of our good Norwich breeders will let you have a pair or two upon which you can at least build up your basic ideas and become critical. Always be critical of your birds, never complacent, or you will find the other fellow will outstrip you.

Mark time with your trial stock. Do not burden yourself with too many birds, because you will probably be disposed to start afresh with experience, and it is easier to part with all, except a possible best, when you have only a few.

From here onwards I propose to treat our subject as if you are a beginner, as indeed I hope you are, your thoughts not trammelled with preconceived ideas. Perhaps you are one who is returning, or who intends to return, to this grand variety. Or maybe you are a practising breeder making but little headway, or possibly a champion just unable to strike the top grade.

Whatever the position, I suggest you maintain an open mind and that you marshal your thoughts anew, as if you are actually a genuine beginner. And let me impress indelibly on your mind that you must have tenacity of purpose, feel confident of your powers, be determined to compete with the best of our breeders, even now, as a beginner.

CHAPTER II

THE IDEAL BIRD

QUITE reasonably you may wonder whether breeding good Norwich Plainheads is necessarily a long process. Definitely I can tell you, no—not if you are an apt student of all that has been written so far, and of that which follows. Good Norwich you will then surely breed, but you will learn that it is the superlatively good that are so difficult to produce.

It is the superlative Norwich Canary, relatively few and far between, which fires the ambition and sustains the keenest interest of our best fanciers. It will be decidedly encouraging, however, for you to know that occasionally novices have beaten all the champion exhibits at some of our open shows, with young Norwich of their own breeding.

At a King's Lynn show held some years back, a Mr. Chilvers, then a novice, was awarded best in show with a young buff cock which thereafter succeeded continuously in the champion section. A Mr. Perkins, at Cambridge, triumphed with a young clear yellow hen, and repeatedly she gathered " best in show " awards at later events.

A Mr. Beale scored highest honours at Clapham with an unflighted yellow cock which, unfortunately for him, was claimed by a champion exhibitor. This bird, in three years' showing, was only once defeated.

Again, there was a novice exhibitor at Bishop's Stortford Show some years back. I cannot recall his

85

name, but he captured the premier award at this exhibition with a neck-grizzled young buff hen. This hen I promptly claimed for myself, but relinquished the claim on the owner informing me that he very badly needed her himself. That novice was very convincing, but I had the mortification of seeing this same hen win countless victories in a champion's hands.

I have given these specific instances—many more could be recalled—to show there is no fluke in these matters, and to convince you thoroughly that novices *can* make the top grade. Why not you?

The Ultimate Aim

By now you are imbued, I hope, with the true fancier spirit, so your ultimate aim, therefore, is to breed Norwich like the bird which figures as a frontispiece to this book. Incidentally, of course, you will gather your harvest of winners and near-winners, but all the time your true objective will be the ideal bird. You intend to improve and continue improving upon your stock until you succeed.

I have always maintained that in order to excel in our birds one must be able to see beauty, or the lack of it, in outline, and especially in detail. Cultivate the artistic within you and never will you be content with Norwich that satisfy humdrum, desultory breeders. Look again and again at the above-mentioned picture; keep it before you while I enumerate its virtues and make my comments, and disagree with me if you can.

That grand head, be it noted, is not over-big, not tremendous, but proportionately bold, and round—a noble head. Its curves, as it lifts from off the beak over and into the back-skull, and across, all so skilfully conveyed by the artist, make one glorious, harmonious, arresting whole.

The eye is strikingly bold, the beak in neat conformity, the cheeks are full, all contributing factors to the undeniable appeal of such a head. Do we see such desirable heads among the Norwich on our show benches? Yes, but not enough of them. Many there are that are bigger, mostly unduly wide and flat in skull; an abundance of heads good in profile but lacking width. Some are good in back-skull but mean in rise and/or expanse of forehead; other heads are disproportionately small.

Abnormal size in head has been an overwhelming passion with many Norwich breeders of the past, a craze which I have steadfastly combated. Generally, these breeders succeeded only in producing the unlovely, that is, heads with excessive feather that surged over the sides to obscure the eyes. Or the cheeks would be so chock-full of feather as to sandwich the eyes into mere slits, sometimes the eyes being almost invisible.

I cannot say to-day that you should not have, or buy, such birds, because they may be well endowed with strong Norwich attributes in other parts of their bodies. For that matter, they may constitute the only suitable material available for you to fashion correctly.

While on this point, I feel I must emphasize that never should we have only a one-track mind with our Norwich. Never should we condemn them, nor praise them, in respect of any one feature. That is how crazes are born. If the head, or any other property, is not as we desire, it is then that our skill and understanding of our subject comes into operation. We have to use such modifying birds as we possess, or secure them where we can.

I am a confirmed believer that cocks play the major part in quality of head, and for that reason I am far keener on good heads in cocks than in hens, But, naturally, I always endeavour to make good head a constant factor on both sides of all my pairings.

You may own, or be offered, cocks with heads such as I have considered undesirable, and of these I would earnestly advise you to have none that come within the last two categories—those with pinched entrance, or with heads disproportionately small. The rest, however, can be complemented by hens that are clean-featured in head properties, not those of mean head, mark you, but hens without a superabundance of head-feather.

The heads of such cocks will prevail in most of the young, not necessarily transmitting the excessive feather detractions, but certainly the actual skull dimensions. From among these, select for your future breeding programme those which show the desired trend to the handsome, bold, classical head, especially the young cocks. Never relax in your efforts. The less likeable head will probably persist for two or more generations, but if your persistence is greater, you will succeed.

Now we will review together the general outline of our handsome modern Plainhead, portrayed by Mr. R. A. Vowles. Mind you, a lot depends on our ability to equip, mentally, our picture bird with life and action, although no artist has ever succeeded better in conveying such an impression of vigour and style.

Cogitate for a while on the body structure, and you will see, as I do, how in general outline our Norwich can be described as of such breadth and depth, within a minimum of length, as to permit of the whole harmonising in perfect curves. These curves converge cleanly at the tail, which, you should observe, is rather short and rigidly in line with the back. The whole is surmounted by that bold, handsome head, which we have already discussed in detail, and which we now know has to be in keeping with this striking body ensemble.

Well, we have now remarked upon a splendid torso and a magnificent head, and for these to be united to fullest effect a short, thick, rounded neck is obviously called for. As you can see, there is only sufficient neck to permit of a nice run from the back of the head on to the shoulders, and again from a full throat to the upper breast.

The greatest possible breadth in the body of a Norwich Canary implies a comparatively broad back, which, to conform with our idea of the bird beautiful, must be nicely filled all over to give a gently rising curve transversely. And in order to ensure that the body tapers down nicely to the tail the greatest expanse must be in the region of the shoulders, so that the back, when looked at from above, resembles a short, thick wedge.

Excellent width of back and shoulders connotes an expansive, uplifted front, which, when nicely rounded by complete fullness, makes a positive contribution to the appeal of our Norwich. The breast requirements, however, have to be considered. The depth must be such as to permit of a downward sweep to the under tail-coverts in one full curve. The full realization comes to us that it is the happiest combination of dimensions which creates the impression of a sturdy, tidily waisted, grandly moulded bird.

Now for the wings and tail as parts of the contour of the perfect Norwich. Both wings and tail simply must be in keeping with the impression already created of a well-moulded, thick-set frame. Necessarily, then, the wings should be quite short and closely braced upon the back, every flight feather in alignment, no dropping of the secondaries, and with the primaries meeting tip to tip on the rump. Only such flights as these can preserve the trim contour of a really smart, stoutly built Norwich.

The tail, too, must also be short, carried well up as if in continuation of the back line so as to give further distinctiveness to a grand body. To do this most effectively it should be reasonably narrow throughout its short length, and tightly packed.

We cannot help but admire this conception of the ideal shape, build, or " type," as it is usually termed among fanciers.

And do we see this grand style of body among the Norwich on our show benches? Yes, frequently, but it seems that excellence in this respect is more general among Scottish Plainheads, though often noted in the Midlands also.

I feel I must counsel all newcomers to the Norwich Fancy to visit the National Exhibition at Olympia if possible, for there alone can they enjoy the exceptional opportunity of comparing Norwich Plainheads from all parts of the kingdom.

Not too hard upon our susceptibility are those Norwich, generally short in build, but with a " dropped " chest—the " duck-bodied," as the late Thomas Pope used to describe them. They are certainly attractive in themselves, comfortable looking, but they compare unfavourably when up against the correctly endowed example.

Many examples can be seen that strike you as being longer than desirable, and naturally, also, they seem long in flights and tail. As often as not they are nicely cleaned out, well across the perch in their " travel," and on a plane level with the eyes, when you see the body in profile only, they make quite impressive specimens. What they really lack is the comparable girth required : their apparent size is in length only. Somewhat " barrelled " is the usual term applied to such Norwich as these.

Now, to my mind, both kinds of these not-so-good Norwich can be improved upon if you have, or can obtain, suitable mates for them. Contrary to what some may think, the seemingly too adipose, comfortable type cannot be paired to advantage with the "barrelled." Both owe their departure from the true type to the same reason—lack of width at the shoulders.

It is the correct set of the shoulders that determines whether the desired formation of body can possibly result, and further, this property in the breeding hens is the quicker road to its achievement. You will remember my earlier remark that our established breeders know good hens to be the keystone of their success. Now you understand why.

Secure the correctly shouldered hens, no matter if small and rather expensive. Don't let the " grass grow under your feet " in making such purchases. You will also remember my earlier observation that probably you will have to *breed* your best hens, better birds than you can ever hope to *buy*. In the interests of breeders this point must be emphasized.

But get the best you can, maybe the little *good* ones, as were my two yellow hens, if you remember, and you can expect, as I do, that bigger *good* young hens will turn up for the next year's breeding. As to the price to be paid, while I am in strong disagreement with fantastic prices, it is valuable advice I give you when I declare a good hen to be worth far more than a comparatively good cock.

The price of an unusually good hen, and they *are* to be had, would be justifiably high, not because of the law of supply and demand, nor because of the seed situation, but because such a hen is probably the product of years of careful breeding. Promising hens, however, are good enough, and they will " produce the goods," make no mistake about that, perhaps not in one year, but certainly in two, three, or four years.

You may find that you are unable to get a really desirable hen. Do not despair, but turn your efforts to securing a good-shouldered cock. Almost of a certainty will he bless your persistence by breeding a hen of the right kind, perhaps two, and your bed-rock foundation for typical Norwich will have arrived only one season later than you wished.

All I have here said is an exemplification of the old fanciers' adage, " Hens for type," but that does not imply that we can be indifferent to the type of the cocks. Similarly, as in our quest for improved heads, so in due course must we endeavour to have the desired type on both sides of all our pairings.

And now for those failings in body structure that cannot be tolerated in birds we buy in. There are some

Norwich Canaries which have " hinged " or drooping tails; others are loose or splayed in tail. In such specimens you will observe a sad transformation from the handsome Norwich to a decidedly graceless-looking Canary.

Some Plainheads can be occasionally seen with humped or " roached " backs. They, likewise, are not at all pleasing to the eye or useful in the breeding cage. Both these faults are among the hardest to eradicate when once they have been introduced into your stock. Try as you will by careful pairing, they will recur in succeeding generations with annoying frequency. Definitely I advise you to have none of them.

Well, enough about type. Let us now bring our thoughts to bear on the pleasingly assertive stance of our picture Norwich. You should note that there is more of the body in front of than behind the legs; in other words, that the legs are well set back. The correct positioning of the legs in a Norwich Plainhead Canary gives greater prominence to that splendid breast— makes the most of it by thrusting that part of the anatomy well over the perch.

This desirable position of the legs, coupled with the fact that they are always set like bent elbows, is conducive to a distinctive, " bouncing " style when our Norwich is in action. The legs have to be short and stout to be in keeping with the rest of our ideal bird, but not *too* short, or away goes the vigorous, bouncing style into a dumpy travel between the perches— " hugging the perches," as it is termed. If too long, a stilty effect would ensue, with " too much daylight between bird and perch," as breeders say. Where I have observed this defect in exhibits it seems that such legs are usually badly positioned also, thus causing a peculiar high, horizontal carriage of the body.

Of the two faults (too short or too long in legs) the former can be successfully dealt with by a generation or two of correct pairing, not more, if your birds are not from consistently bred dumpy stock. A bird with long legs, however, I would not consider for a moment. This is a defect that is altogether foreign to the concepts of a good Norwich, and probably introduced at some time by a " don't care " breeder.

Now we have arrived at a stage in which we have become fully conversant with the required physical attributes of our Norwich Plainhead. But, consciously or subconsciously, we have, throughout, envisaged our bird with plumage complete, sartorially correct, so to speak, and displaying the robust figure to perfection. Plumage so compact, so close-fitting, that it really established for us every one of those eminently desirable properties we have discussed—the moulded head and full neck, those sweeping curves across and under the neat waist, and that trim cutaway.

In the living Norwich, this close feather should strike you as being wondrously soft and silky, lustrously rich in colour, and having a " life " indicative not only of good breeding, but of perfect condition. In short, nothing but the finest raiment is fitting for such a noble bird as a tip-top Norwich Canary.

But it is in respect to feather that many of our old breeders failed. They achieved the proportional build and bold head, yet, as one might say, they arrayed their Norwich in fustian rather than glorious silk. In Fancy parlance, their Norwich may have excelled in type, but quality, as revealed in texture and colour of the feather, was ordinary.

As regards the texture of the feather, close, soft and silky, I say unhesitatingly that lack of such quality plumage was due to ignorance of feather properties. Many of our old fanciers knew not what they were doing. The vogue then was size, and more size, and in order to gain more *apparent* size, continuous double-buffing was rife. The loss of a clean-moulded contour was bad enough, but, as it transpired, a worse evil befell the breed, the still-dreaded " lumps."

For both reasons, our best breeders have for some years past rigidly adhered to the orthodox pairing—yellow to buff, or *vice versa*. To the second evil this sensible procedure, and the destruction of lump-affected birds when they did appear, have made our grand variety far less prone than of yore.

You will remember I ascertained that my new birds were from stocks that had not been double-buffed or double-yellowed for several generations back. Perhaps you may not be quite so well assured with your new stock, but I think that probably you will, because there has been a proportionately greater number of yellows available during recent years. Buffs predominated very largely in the bad old days, yellows being extremely scarce.

CHAPTER III

YELLOWS, BUFFS AND CINNAMONS

IF you are a beginner you have probably wondered what precisely is meant by the terms " yellow " and " buff," so before we proceed further, I will enlighten you on this matter.

These terms indicate the two *orders*, not the colours, of feather that you will meet with in all Canaries. I prefer the synonymous terms, " jonque " and " mealy," because they are not so misleading to a beginner, although " jonque," from the French, implies jonquil-coloured.

Nature equips her birds separately with these two *kinds* of feather, so that in the average course of promiscuous pairings between a given species the balance of plumage shall be maintained. Any deterioration, therefore, in the feather of our Canaries can only be attributed to the misjudgment of breeders, and indiscriminate double-buffing undoubtedly comes within this indictment.

The " yellow " order of feather is the thinner in web, and the colour, be it yellow, green, cinnamon, or blue, travels right to the tip of the feather. As a result, a " yellow " bird, in all species, shows its colour to its full depth and richness.

The " buff " order is stouter in web, and the colour, whatever its hue, stops short of the tip of the feathers, and a light fringe is thus formed to each. The outcome

96

in the usual buff Canary is a subjugation of its real colour by an overlay of this light fringing. In the ideal buff, however, the colour is still rich on the head, back, and breast, beautifully imbricated by those light fringes.

But let me emphasize that one order of feather is comparatively thin, and the other stout. Think on this for a moment. Quite obviously, it appears to you, nature meant one order of feather to complement the other in the procreation of our Canaries, that is, " yellow " paired to " buff." Yet many unthinking fanciers of old, by persistent double-buffing, in the craze for more apparent size, crowded increasingly stouter and denser feather on the same area of skin surface.

But Nature was not mocked. She gave her harsh verdict in " graining " of plumage, loss of shapeliness, loose feather at flanks and tail coverts, head-feather that obscured the eyes.

Those days are now past, or passing, but occasionally you can still hear a jubilant winner proclaiming his exhibit to be from a double-buff mating. Don't be misled into thinking the process to be the open sesame to success, and proceed to do likewise. That winning exhibitor, you will note, does not speak about the unsatisfactory nest mates, nor does he inform you next season that his breeding programme has gone awry, that his Norwich are wearing " trousers," etc.

Mind you, double-buffing can be justified in certain circumstances in other varieties, but in Norwich, I maintain, in view of so much done in the past, it is not only unnecessary but actually harmful.

The introduction of cinnamon " blood " is often advocated to remedy a lessening in quality of feather, but it is no miracle worker on a really poor order of plumage. I certainly agree that it has a great refining influence, but no small share of that virtue can be accredited to the rigid necessity in cinnamon breeding to adhere to orthodox pairing, with, perhaps, an occasional need for double-yellowing, but no double-buffing.

There is a strong temptation to court the cinnamon influence when one observes the beautiful *rich* cinnamon marking and variegation among notable winners, but extreme care must be exercised if you wish your Norwich to compare with them. Remember, too, those exceptional winners were, above all things, outstanding Plainheads, and their markings a lovely incidental.

There are, of course, some grandly typical Cinnamon Norwich, but the cinnamon enthusiasts of to-day need them badly, and such as they are likely to part with will not serve us well in type, head, or wings. Apart from this, I am definitely against an introduction from any Cinnamon Norwich stud, for a very strong reason.

Nobody admires a rich cinnamon variegation or appreciates cinnamon quality better than myself, but the time for me to indulge in my liking will not arrive until my stock has become firmly established in structural and *colour* potential. I earnestly advise this same course to you. Later you will appreciate my advice the better when you are more adept with increasing experience.

When the time comes, my introduction will be by way of a good cinnamon-variegated hen from a painstaking Plainhead breeder. Probably he will be as ready to part with one as I was in my past Norwich career, and for the same reason.   This is not only the best, but the logical course of action.

I shall find quite ten reasonably good hens available, as against one possibly indifferent cinnamon-variegated cock.   Again, I can expect a cock from my improved

Beautiful example of a cinnamon Norwich Plainhead with exquisite texture of feather and attractive markings. Cinnamons are well worth cultivating.

and now established stock to prevail in the extremities (head, wings, tail) of the young, points to be carefully watched where cinnamon is concerned.

If my birds are purely green-bred, I shall get no cinnamon evidenced in the progeny.   But some of the young cocks will be carriers for cinnamon, and an occasional cinnamon-variegated hen should appear from them in the following season.

Straightway will I dispose of that cinnamon-variegated hen when she has produced, say, two suitable young cocks. And readily, too, will I dispose of those bred by me, if cinnamon results become too frequent in my stud. I definitely do not want cinnamon characteristics to predominate in my Plainhead stock, which is a pronounced colour breed, *for cinnamon is certainly a colour-reducing agent.*

Nor do I wish to see a number of self cinnamons cropping up. To use them, however typical, as breeders would increase the cinnamon permeation, and further weaken the ground colour of my established stock. Those beautiful cinnamon markings, with me, must occur fortuitously.

CHAPTER IV

COLOUR AND SIZE

WE will now discuss the development and maintenance of good colour in Plainheads. You may remember I mentioned earlier that every bird in my new stock was to some degree variegated, and I imagine not a few established breeders looked wise when they read that statement. Probably they surmised that I should get all dark and heavily variegated progeny, without a single clear bird—and so did I.

I am able to say, however, that I bred some very promising youngsters from these variegated parents. Three foul greens were among them, but the anticipated "circus horses" proved to be all pleasingly lightly variegated, and, surprising as it may seem to some, one pairing which produced two of the greens gave also a clear and a ticked.

But even if my initial stock had not produced a solitary clear, I should not have been in the least concerned about it.

You must realize that I am in the same position as you are, or will be, that is, building up from the very beginning, and, as in all other requirements, I wish colour to be on a firm foundation. I must know where I stand regarding this most important essential in first-rate Norwich Plainheads. Throughout the centuries, Norwich have been bred for colour, and lack of rich colour cannot be made good by colour-feeding.

Seemingly contradictory to this statement, it is worth mentioning that I have occasionally had some almost colourless youngsters in years gone by which have moulted a fiery-red on colour-food. But every such bird was strictly green-bred, and I cannot help but attribute the phenomenon to this fact. I feel sure green " blood " gives a peculiar virtue to the pigmentation properties, undeveloped in nature, but revealed by colour-feeding, which is, in fact, colour addition.

However, I am fairly certain such gratifying results from colour-feeding will never occur where clear is persistently bred to clear for generations in a fanatical desire for clear birds only. I know the clear Norwich is often referred to as the pinnacle of attainment, but let us examine this point together and get a true perspective on it.

Dark Underflue

Clear Norwich, in themselves, evidence the elimination of dark pigment, although were you to blow up the under-feathers of a clear derived from sound colour breeding you would find plenty of intensely dark underflue. Breeders know this to be indicative of good colouring properties and of high colour-breeding potential.

Pair such clears to similar clears, retaining only the clears for successive breeding (always provided they are good in other respects), and for a season or two you will get some pleasingly good-coloured clears. But from here on you should watch your step.

Persist with this procedure a season or so more, and the loss of the dark pigment (or shall we call it the enriching element?) will become rapid, until you find the dark underflue has paled, or is absent, and the colour generally of your stock failing.

When I visit a room where variegated birds are conspicuously absent, inevitably I observe also that the general colour of the stock leaves much to be desired.

We are told that " green blood is the fount of colour," and we shall certainly come to appreciate the truth of this dictum as time goes on. This does not mean, however, that you must necessarily have self or foul-green Norwich. A reservoir of green blood as represented in a good sprinkling of variegateds is all that is necessary.

They should be birds intensely rich in their variegation, not of the " mousey " tone, such as one sees in " throw-ups " from some strain in which the breeding of clears has long been persisted in.

" But," you may say, " practically *all* your youngsters are variegateds." That is so. But the clears will come, and, what is more to the point, I shall know whence they came.

While on this aspect of Plainhead culture, it is amazing how many variegateds win premier honours at the shows. So why worry if you don't get an abundance of clears?

Be steadfast in your pursuit of type and quality, and always tolerant of variegation, realizing its valuable contribution to colour. You will receive due recompense on the show benches, and those clears that you certainly will breed later on will be as hot as fire.

It has been my experience that variegated birds are to a marked degree more vigorous than the usual order of clears. The cocks seem lustier in song, more assertive in carriage, and far more satisfactory as good progeny-getting sires. The hens are usually more bustling in the stock cage and more businesslike in the breeding cage, when five eggs per clutch occur with gratifying frequency.

Of course, the foregoing is contingent upon your purchases coming from healthy, virile studs and upon the subsequent feeding and attention given to them. With these provisos, variegation always connotes greater vigour as well as colour maintenance—a logical viewpoint when one reflects that clearness, which means loss of pigmentary properties, can reasonably be associated with organic deficiencies.

Vigour a Prime Essential

Without vigour, however good your Norwich are reputed to be, no breeding headway can be made. Planning for the seasons to come would be futile, and the development of a strain by inter-breeding and, ultimately, by inbreeding, hopeless.

Do take this fundamental fact seriously to heart. Vigour is a prime essential, and you *must* have it from the beginning if you hope for lasting enjoyment and success with your Norwich. Size is no criterion of vigour; many over-big Norwich are definitely lethargic.

Whatever their size, seek only Norwich of type and quality, such as I have described, with firm, " alive " plumage, braced flights, and an obvious readiness to flip from perch to perch.

Size in Norwich. At last we have got to a question which, I imagine, has been revolving in my readers' minds for some time. Let us get down to discussing it.

In my novice days I used to dream of Norwich as big as pigeons; but they were only dreams. In reality

I knew even then that size, consistent with type and quality, must have definite limits.

Size, or the lack of it, was the all-pervading concern of Norwich breeders in those far-off days, and it worked havoc in our ranks. We know better to-day. In bygone years show reports would refer to winning exhibits in such terms as "massive," "of great substance," "Goliath," "Mammoth," "Jumbo," "Shire-horse," and so on.

Naturally, the bulk of our breeders came to think that size was the *sine qua non* in exhibition Norwich. Definitely it is not, and really it never has been. Size of itself, real or apparent, is no great accomplishment. I could, regardless of the real and finer essentials, establish size in all my stock in three to four years, and find no difficulty in so doing.

Have you ever noticed that the best Norwich in show is, more often than not, a quality bird of medium size only? "But," you will say, "surely a big good one will always beat a little or medium-sized good one?" Yes, if they came big *and good*.

The finest big Norwich I have ever seen was a young buff cock exhibited by Mr. J. E. Hartup (Accrington) in 1928—the best bird in the tremendous Liverpool and Bradford shows of that year. That cock was a spanking good Norwich.

A few years later, in 1932, Mr. Hartup won a hot class of twenty-eight at the "Palace" with a medium-sized buff hen, smaller than most in her class. She also was marvellously good. Do you get the idea? Whether large, medium or small, your bird must be a real Norwich, possessing all the main characteristics.

The judges will look for these essentials before they even consider size. That is how it has been all the time, though there have been periods when breeders foolishly exhibited their outsize birds instead of those displaying all-round merit.

A measure of size in good Norwich is undoubtedly a telling factor, but only in *good* Norwich. I have mentioned one big bird only, exhibited over twenty years ago, as fully measuring up to the term " big good one." I have heard about, but never seen, another celebrated big Norwich, exhibited by Mr. W. C. Hernon. This bird, I believe, remained unbeaten during three successive show seasons (1942-4).

It must be obvious, therefore, that big and really good Norwich are exceptional, and that, as I have already said, the best, as a rule, are of medium size only.

Never should I think of striving for the outsize specimen at the expense of much that really counts in good Norwich, especially quality of feather and clean-moulded shape. I know from past experience that I shall get occasional birds plenty big enough to please the most exacting, consistent with type and quality. The rest of my Norwich will be of average good medium size.

Greatly assisted by Mr. Vowles' splendid drawing, I have conveyed to you all that constitutes a good Plainhead, and endeavoured to enlighten you on how to breed high-class exhibition birds. Top-notchers are, of course, very few and far between. This has always been so, and perhaps it is just as well. If perfect Plainheads were common there would be no real sense of achievement in breeding them, no scope for skill.

Let me impress upon breeders the great importance of exhibiting their best birds in order to determine the extent to which they have actually succeeded. Progress, name and fame will never be enjoyed if the cream of the show examples are kept at home.

Green Norwich Canary, rich grass green in colour and with appropriate markings.

Too many breeders have an altogether wrong outlook in regard to shows. They seem to sense only the competitive element at these events, are overwhelmed by it, and become shy and hesitant. They fail to realize that, above all things, the shows help us correctly to appraise our birds, and to gauge our rate of yearly progress with them.

I have met this peculiar complex in fanciers again and again—the all-too-modest individuals who always *think* their birds are never good enough for the show benches. Let me relate quite a remarkable instance of this undue modesty which may serve to banish a most unfortunate complex from the minds of those who suffer from it.

In 1929 I judged a very fine members' show at St. Albans, and in my enthusiasm I told the secretary that among the Norwich were some of the best I had seen that year. As an outcome, I was duly introduced to their owner, Mr. Dennison, and we adjourned to a nearby hotel.

"What do you really think of my Norwich, Mr. Smith?" was his inevitable question. "Show your young birds at the 'Palace,'" I replied encouragingly "No, no," he said, "they are not good enough for the 'Palace.' I only entered them here to help our show." Without hesitation I informed him that from what I had seen of his birds they should win at the "Palace." He looked askance at me, but, being aware of the fact that I was drinking nothing stronger than lemonade, he said, "Very well, I will, since you think so highly of them."

His young yellow cock proved to be the National Norwich cup winner, his yellow hen was fourth in her class, while his two buff hens gained first and second prizes! But for my conversation with this fancier, those young Norwich would have been denied the great honours due to them, their praises remained unsung.

Every serious breeder of Norwich, or any other exhibition breed, for that matter, should make a special point of visiting as many of the larger shows as possible, there to develop their ideas and to fraternize with those with whom they intend to compete later on. It is these exhibitions which may well provide the most favourable opportunities to make contact with those breeders best able to give you a good start.

Later come the comparatively localized open shows, and the various clubs' annual shows. Competition will be easier at these fixtures, but here again don't miss the opportunities for comparison. Only thus will you discover unsuspected failures in your birds. The novice should avoid the development of a parochial outlook. Never let him over-estimate the merits of a local winning bird. Always regard your Norwich and your skill as being good enough to compete with any breeder. If you adopt this attitude, then you will be almost certain to breed good Norwich, and, incidentally, plenty of winners.

Before proceeding to the subject of how to make the most of our birds for the show bench, it may be necessary to remind young fanciers that they will have different orders in their Plainheads—cocks and hens, yellows and buffs, marked, variegated and clear birds. To bring this matter up may, perhaps, seem quite unnecessary, but I know from wide experience how so·many of our breeders develop a preference for big yellow cocks, shall we say, whereas a marked, medium-sized buff hen, or a smaller yellow hen, may be equally likely to bring home the red tickets. Remember, it is type and quality we and our judges seek, irrespective of sex, size or variegation, every time and all the time.

Let me record another little story in order to impress this on your mind. Northampton show drew a marvellous Norwich entry in 1938, and at this fixture a novice queried why I made his rather small variegated buff hen best novice Norwich in show over his more imposing clear buff cock, which had twice achieved the same honour at previous events. It was the hen's first outing, by the way. I explained at great length, but he was obviously unconvinced, so I terminated the discussion—forgetting he had that day graduated into champion status—by telling him to show the hen at the next National.

On my rounds of the great Horticultural Hall I had the pleasure of seeing that same bonny little hen standing fourth in a strong champion class of twenty-five. The buff cock, by no means disgraced, was cardless in a class of fifteen. That erstwhile novice may possibly read this, but I know that never again will he develop a one-bird mentality. Neither will you, I trust.

CHAPTER V

TRAINING FOR EXHIBITION

I FEEL sure that the majority of breeders will show the complete range of their Norwich as far as is possible, and thereby learn where their strength really lies. With this decision in mind, it becomes imperative that every one of the season's youngsters should be run into a show cage and carefully studied.

Obviously it is necessary to get them accustomed to a show cage, to being closely examined, and trained to pose to the best advantage. Some breeders cut a hole cleanly in the back of a few old show cages and by means of two screw-hooks suitably positioned in the back, hang them on the wire fronts of their stock cages so that the hole coincides with the door of the latter. The young birds quickly find their way into these show cages and become accustomed to the more restricted space. A few titbits can be used to encourage entry.

Undoubtedly when you handle your Norwich, as I invariably do, you must have confidence in your ability to do so without harm to bird or plumage. I always catch up my young Norwich and place them in their show cages for inspection as soon as they are well developed, say, at about six weeks. This is done on every possible occasion, quite unhurriedly and confidently. After the initial scare they soon learn that I intend them no harm, and usually they will conveniently remain on the perch and allow me quietly to take

111

them from it. If in the show cage a bird is unsteady in the early stages, I place that show cage at an angle to another, the inmate of which is more tractable. Very soon the first bird acquires better manners.

When you are cleaning out your cages, or engaged in some other activity in the birdroom, never fail to place your prospective exhibits in their show cages. Your passing to and fro does much to steady them. Another tip is to place the show cages in different positions on successive occasions. You will readily understand that in a show hall your exhibits will be subjected to all sorts of strange sights, so you must do all you can in the birdroom to get them accustomed to changed surroundings.

And that brings me to another point in the training of Norwich. Don't take it too hardly if they fail to do you justice when first exhibited. I have won cups with Norwich which could not gain second, third or fourth prizes at their initial outing. They developed stage-fright in the new and vast surroundings of their first show, and seemed nothing like so good as they appeared in the birdroom. The experience, however, completed their training, and subsequently they played their parts right well.

Training Norwich and all other Canaries means getting them used to show cages and show conditions, but if your birds are to excel at the exhibitions that will not be enough; you must display them to the best possible advantage. Superior birds deserve superior frames to set them off, in other words, spick and span show cages.

It can be assumed that for the early shows your Norwich will be spotlessly clean—in the pristine glory of their newly moulted plumage. For the later shows you will have to wash them, or get an experienced exhibitor to wash them for you.

Norwich show cages are simply box-cages, with wire front, two perches, and a door at the side. The interior is treated with Aspinall's " Hedge Sparrow Egg Tint " enamel, the exterior being black and the outside of the drinker also black. The flooring, in normal times is covered with canary seed. It is quite a simple style of cage,

Norwich Show Cage

you will agree, and strictly utilitarian, yet definitely the best for the purpose. But you would be amazed at the variety in condition, in colours, and in perches loose, round, square, rough, too thick, or too thin, that will sometimes confront you.

The Scottish Plainhead Club, of which I am proud to be a member, have a rule that exhibits shall be debarred if not in regulation cages. I will not elaborate further, except to say that if Scottish breeders and all our leading exhibitors make a point of conforming to regulations, then, obviously, every Norwich exhibitor should do the same. Common sense dictates that we shall not declare ourselves, by our cages, as not of the best among breeders and exhibitors.

Well, now, experience gained at the shows will have cemented our views, in regard to the quality of our Norwich, so how shall we proceed then?

For myself, I have only a small stock, and although they have bred well, I anticipate that I shall have to seek a bird, or perhaps two, to balance an odd hen or cock that I find I wish to keep because of certain desirable properties. Such purchases *may* not be necessary, for it is surprising how some Plainheads develop beyond expectations, while others disappoint.

If I find it absolutely necessary to introduce fresh blood, I shall exercise the same care as from the beginning, making particularly sure of vigour, and not forgetting to avoid " lump " purveyors like the plague. My matings will always be the best to the best, within the restrictions imposed by orthodox yellow to buff pairing and moderation in variegation. I shall never pair two old birds together. Always mate youth to the aged, say, four years upward in cocks, three years or more in hens. By cross-breeding the progeny you will probably get the desired results.

You may have noticed that I have said nothing about blood relations when future pairings are arranged. Given real vigour in your Norwich, there is nothing to it. In the early stages of developing my stud, I shall be inter-breeding deliberately, and, by chance, I may possibly in-breed with certain pairs. As I have said, this does not worry me at all, for in due course I shall definitely in-breed in order to achieve specific results. But let me warn all breeders that to commence in-breeding before you are possessed of most of the requisite properties in your birds is simply foolish.

On the other hand, when all your stock is found to

be eminently desirable—as a result of most careful selection and elimination—in-breeding is the only method by which you can create a highly satisfactory strain of your own. Then it is that you will consistently breed Norwich, again by selecting the best for successive pairings, that will be homogeneous for all the properties you are so eager to secure and maintain in your stud.

But make no mistake, without due care and understanding of all that has been written in these chapters, you can, by in-breeding, just as surely make your Norwich Plainheads homogeneous for bad features.

Here we arrive at the point of discussing genetics as applied to our Norwich. Many fanciers think it an abstruse science beyond their powers of comprehension, and they become shy about it, brush it aside, as if to say: "We have managed very well all these years without it, and shall continue to do so." This is a sad mistake.

Genetics is a comparatively new science, the application of which is proving of immense benefit to live stock breeders generally. But while you have no need to study genetics as a science, you would be foolish not to apply its discoveries to your breeding operations.

When you have created your strain by inter-breeding, and later by in-breeding, made your Norwich stable, reduced variation to a minimum, then can the truths of genetics help you considerably—enable you better to understand what you are doing, or what you have done. You will discover that despite all your care you may lose a certain esteemed character, or, perhaps, all the time you have been oblivious to some small but vital failing.

CHAPTER VI

ELIMINATING " LUMPS "

WITH reference to that unfortunate malady known as " lumps " which has afflicted Norwich Canaries in the past, I have full confidence in the viewpoint of our genetical scientists that we can breed our Plainheads so that they become disease-resistant.

An unfortunate outbreak of lumps from a believed clean Norwich strain is, to my mind, definitely due to the operation of a certain gene, or the loss of it. For instance, I experienced lumps in my stock of some two hundred and thirty Plainheads in 1922 for the first time. Then, contrary to my outlook to-day, I destroyed the offending buff cock which had been introduced into the stud, his progeny, and their progeny, *most of them without a sign of lumps*—nineteen birds in all.

For seventeen years after that I was free from the scourge, until in 1939 a yellow hen, in her third year, developed a lump. More enlightened by then, I realized that the disease, after all, was latent in my stock, but remarkably dormant. In other words, my Norwich were largely " lump " resistant.

Definitely, lumps are hereditary, and to those unacquainted with genetics as a science, they would appear incapable of eradication. We owe a debt of gratitude to the geneticists. Thanks to them, we now know that this trouble can be overcome.

116

I believe my new stock to be clean, but from experience all I can claim is that they are "lump" resistant, though exactly to what extent I cannot tell. My prevailing idea, and I want it to be yours, also, is how to increase those powers of resistance to the point that my Plainheads can be declared immune.

This is what I am going to do, and every Plainhead breeder in the land can do likewise for the good of the breed and for the satisfaction of accomplishment. I shall obtain three, perhaps four, healthy, vigorous, close-feathered suitable Border hens, and to each of these I shall mate my *best* lump-resistant Norwich cocks —not at any expense to my Plainhead breeding programme, because I shall also run those same cocks with their chosen Norwich partners.

Long-Term Procedure

From the progeny I shall retain those birds showing the desired trend towards Norwich characteristics. Believe me, there will be enough for my purpose, and these I shall breed one to the other, regardless of blood relationship, with an occasional introduction from my Plainheads. This I will do for some three or four years, keeping them absolutely separate from my Norwich stud until, I warrant you, I shall have some likely Norwich immune from lumps. These I shall then breed into my established stud to increase further their powers of resistance.

I shall not stop at this. I shall proceed with my separate line of Border descent as before, with introductions from the progeny of the birds mentioned in the preceding paragraph. Believe me, in the course of a few years my best Plainheads will as likely be found in the one line of breeding as in the other, immune from lumps, and both lines capable of being freely inter-bred with the other.

Mind you, I don't claim this method to be a miracle-worker with lump-prevalent strains, only a modifier of the evil. But even so, with greater patience on a longer course, it will effect a radical cure.

Now, adverting back to the other points, such as the loss of a character, or perhaps the neglect of a failing in your carefully built-up, inbred strain. Geneticists would say of the first that you have lost the gene for that particular feature, or the second, that you must add the necessary gene.

This in plain Fancy parlance means that you must seek an outcross with the required property, and if you obtain it from a painstaking, reputable breeder, not only will it be of general all-round excellence, but in all probability it will be homozygous, or solid in breeding potential, for that feature, which is very much to the good.

However, in other respects, the outcross may introduce some undesirable features, and it is here that the most rudimentary knowledge of applied genetics can save our strains from general collapse, and ourselves from disappointment.

The geneticist explains, and rightly, that in the introduction of our outcross the progeny thus obtained is heterozygous, or, in other words, mixed in breeding potential, not only for the desired feature, but maybe for some that are unwanted. The likelihood of more variations in features which previously we had largely overcome by inbreeding comes into play again, so we have to be careful with our new introduction.

If we are discreet as to whom we approach for our outcross, the resulting young, in all probability, will be excellent. The outcross will have " clicked." Sometimes, however, only Norwich inferior to our own will be the result, but here we have received enlightenment from the geneticists, whereas before we should have thought the experiment had gone hopelessly awry.

Instead of being discouraged and abandoning the results of the outcross, as we might have done, we are now better advised to continue with the best of the young, in the knowledge that they are of mixed breeding potential (heterozygous), and that the hidden, wanted characters will assuredly come to the surface in some of the progeny of subsequent pairings.

Then, with our ordinary ability in selection, and by inbreeding them with a line, or two lines, of our established strain, we shall definitely produce Norwich homozygous for all our previous characters, plus the needed feature.

Of course, the outcross individual Plainhead is obviously superior to our own, and it should be disposed of immediately after its first use, as we certainly would do if it was inferior. To go further with an outcross that gives you any adverse result would mean weeding out too many failings, taking us back to where we began.

Weeding out will almost certainly be found necessary after any new introduction, but it would be foolish to intensify our difficulties in this direction. In order to reduce this weeding process to a minimum, whether an outcross " clicks " or not, only a very few of the most promising of the progeny, perhaps one or two, should be kept for breeding into our established stocks. With such precaution, the temporary instability of our strains will be quickly overcome, and thanks to our careful introduction and procedure with the necessary outcross we should breed better Plainheads than ever before.

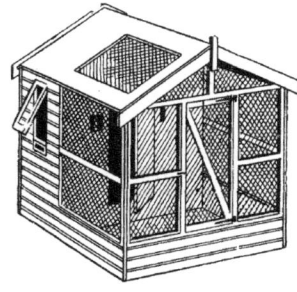

BOOKS ON BIRDKEEPING

BUDGERIGARS

The Cult of the Budgerigar . *By W. Watmough*
Exhibition Budgerigars . *By Dr. M. D. S. Armour*
All About Budgerigars . *By F. W. Pratley*
Inbreeding Budgerigars . *By Dr. M. D. S. Armour*
Budgerigar Matings and Colour Expectations . *By F. S. Elliott and E. W. Brooks*
The Budgerigar in Captivity . *By Denys Weston*
Colour Breeding in Budgerigars . *By W. Watmough*
Budgerigar Breeding and Show Register . *By W. Watmough*
Budgerigars and How to Breed Them . *By Cyril Rogers*
Talking Budgerigars and How to Train Them . *By Andrew Wilson*
Budgerigar Breeders' Pedigree Forms
Homing Budgerigars . *The Duke of Bedford*

CANARIES

Guide to Canary Breeding and Exhibiting . *By W. E. Brooks*
Canary Breeding for Beginners . *By Claude St. John*
The Roller Canary . *By H. W. Gutierrez*
The Border Fancy Canary . *By James Patterson*
Canary Breeding Room Register
The Yorkshire Canary . *By Shackleton*
Cinnamon Inheritance in Canaries . *By A. K. Gill*
The Lizard Canary . *By G. T. Dodwell*

BRITISH BIRDS

Breeding British Birds in Aviaries and Cages . *By H. Norman*
Mules and Hybrids . *By Rosslyn Mannering*

FOREIGN BIRDS

Foreign Birds for Beginners . *By D. H. S. Risdon*
Foreign Birds for Garden Aviaries . *By Alec Brooksbank*
Lovebirds and Parrotlets . *By L. P. Luke*

GENERAL

Aviaries, Birdrooms and Cages . *By L. P. Luke and Allen Silver*
Wild Plants and Seeds for Birds . *By R. Morse*
Questions Answered About Cage Birds. *By Andrew Dick*
Bird Ailments and Accidents . *By Claude St. John*

Any of these books may be obtained through Booksellers or direct from the Publishers :

POULTRY WORLD LTD., DORSET HOUSE, STAMFORD ST., LONDON, S.E.I.

CATALOGUE GIVING CONTENTS AND PRICES ON REQUEST

9 781528 702492